Christmas

The Annual of Christmas Literature and Art

Christmas

Christmas

The Annual of Christmas Literature and Art

Volume Fifty-seven

Augsburg Publishing House
Minneapolis, Minnesota

Table of Contents

In this volume...

CHRISTMAS marks the anniversary of the greatest gift ever given—God's Son, Jesus Christ. The few short verses with which the New Testament writers construct the account of this gift-giving include references to the rich and the poor, to gifts concrete and spiritual, and they encompass such themes as hope, joy, love, and peace.

No story has so moved the human heart to respond in kind. God loved, we love; God gave, we give. At the Advent season, with the imminent retelling of the Christmas story, the human heart is reborn to generosity.

This year marks the 75th anniversary of the death of William Booth, who founded an organization that has become an incarnation of God's giving spirit. "A Time for Giving" on page 14 highlights the Christmas activities of The Salvation Army and sets the theme for this, the 57th volume of CHRISTMAS.

The touching story, "A Sunny Christmas," page 18, reveals a couple who, in the spirit of Christmas, opened their home only to find that their hearts also were captured.

Lois Rand's "The Giving Heart" on page 57 identifies the relationship between the Christmas gospel and the motives of the human heart as a theme common to the stories we have come to love as classics.

The article on Christmas seals, "Biggest Little Thing in the World," page 39, outlines how one man's Christmas response focused on health and life, providing a way virtually to eliminate tuberculosis.

Six new carols, pages 30-37, reflect the efforts of poets and musicians to set this theme to music.

On page 23, art historian Phillip Gugel comments on a nativity painting by Rogier van der Weyden in which the artist positions his patron with those gathered at the Bethlehem manger. In another era such patronage was considered a response of the human heart.

It is the prayer of the editors that in this volume the focus on the response of the human heart to the Christmas gospel will open for you the true meaning of Christmas.

Editorial staff: Leonard Flachman, Karen Walhof, Jennifer Fast, Kristine Oberg; Richard Hillert, music consultant.

The Christmas Story

The Christmas Story
According to St. Luke and St. Matthew

And in the sixth month the angel Gabriel was sent from God to a city of Galilee named Nazareth, to a virgin betrothed to a man whose name was Joseph, of the house of David. And the virgin's name was Mary.

And having come in, the angel said to her, "Hail, highly favored one, the Lord is with you; blessed are you among women!"

And when she saw him, she was troubled at his saying, and considered what manner of greeting this was.

And the angel said to her, "Do not be afraid, Mary, for you have found favor with God. And behold, you will conceive in your womb and bring forth a Son, and shall call his name Jesus. He will be great, and will be called the Son of the Highest; and the Lord God will give him the throne of his father David. And he will reign over the house of Jacob forever, and of his kingdom there will be no end."

Then Mary said to the angel, "How can this be, since I do not know a man?"

And the angel answered and said to her, "The Holy Spirit will come upon you, and the power of the Highest will overshadow you; therefore, also, that Holy One who is to be born will be called the Son of God.

And it came to pass in those days that a decree went out from Caesar Augustus that all the world should be registered. This census first took place while Quirinius was governing Syria. And all went to be registered, everyone to his own city.

And Joseph also went up from Galilee, out of the city of Nazareth, into Judea, to the city of David, which is called Bethlehem, because he was of the house and lineage of David, to be registered with Mary, his betrothed wife, who was with child.

And so it was, that while they were there, the days were completed that she should be delivered. And she brought forth her firstborn Son, and wrapped him in swaddling cloths, and laid him in a manger, because there was no room for them in the inn.

The Christmas Story, printed in Amharic, the national language of Ethiopia

በስድስተኛውም ፡ ወር ፡ መልአኩ ፡ ገብር ኤል ፡ ናዝሬት ፡ ወደምትባል ፡ ወደ ፡ ገሊላ ከተማ ፡ ከዳዊት ፡ ወገን ፡ ለሆነው ፡ ዮሴፍ ለሚባል ፡ ሰው ፡ ወደ ፡ ታጨች ፡ ወደ ፡ እንዲት ፡ ድንግል ፡ ከእግዚአብሔር ፡ ዘንድ ፡ ተላከ ፤ የድ ንግሊ ቱም ፡ ስም ፡ ማርያም ፡ ነበረ ። መልአ ኩም ፡ ወደ ፡ እርስዋ ፡ ገብቶ ፡— ፡ ደስ ፡ ይበል ሽ ፡ ጸጋ ፡ የሞላብሽ ፡ ሆይ ፡ ጌታ ፡ ከአንቺ ፡ ጋር ፡ ነው ፤ አንቺ ፡ ከሴቶች ፡ መካከል ፡ የተባረክሽ ነሽ ፡ አላት ። እርስዋም ፡ ባየችው ፡ ጊዜ ፡ ከን ግግሩ ፡ በጣም ፡ ደነገጠችና ፡— ፡ ይህ ፡ እንዴት ፡ ያለ ፡ ሰላምታ ፡ ነው ? ብላ ፡ አሰበች ። መልአ ኩም ፡ እንዲህ ፡ አላት ፡— ፡ ማርያም ፡ ሆይ ÷ በእ ግዚአብሔር ፡ ፊት ፡ ጸጋ ፡ አግኝተሻልና ፡ አት

ፍሪ ። እነሆም ÷ ትፀንሻለሽ ፡ ወንድ ፡ ልጅም ፡ ትወልጃለሽ ÷ ስሙንም ፡ ኢየሱስ ፡ ትዲዋለሽ ። እርሱ ፡ ታላቅ ፡ ይሆናል ፡ የልዑል ፡ ልጅም ፡ ይባላል ÷ ጌታ ፡ አምላክም ፡ የአባቱን ፡ የዳዊትን ፡ ዙፋን ፡ ይሰጠዋል ፤ በያዕቆብ ፡ ቤትም ፡ ላይ ፡ ለዘላለም ፡ ይነግሣል ÷ ለመንግሥቱም ፡ መጨ ረሻ ፡ የለውም ። ማርያምም ፡ መልአኩን ፡— ፡ ወንድ ፡ ስለማላውቅ ፡ ይህ ፡ እንዴት ፡ ይሆናል ? አለችው ። መልአኩም ፡ መለስ ፡ እንዲህ ፡ አላት ፡— ፡ መንፈስ ፡ ቅዱስ ፡ በአንቺ ፡ ላይ ፡ ይመ ጣል ÷ የልዑልም ፡ ኃይል ፡ ይጸልልሻል ፤ ስለ ዚህ ፡ ደግሞ ፡ ከአንቺ ፡ የሚወለደው ፡ ቅዱሱ ፡ የእግዚአብሔር ፡ ልጅ ፡ ይባላል ።

በዚያም ፡ ወራት ፡ ዓለም ፡ ሁሉ ፡ እንዲጻፍ ፡ ከአውግስጦስ ፡ ቄሣር ፡ ትእዛዝ ፡ ወጣች ። ቄሬ ኒዎስ ፡ በሶርያ ፡ አገር ፡ ገዥ ፡ በነበረ ፡ ጊዜ ፡ ይህ ፡ የመጀመሪያ ፡ ጽሕፈት ፡ ሆነ ። ሁሉም ፡ እያን ዳንዱ ፡ ይጻፍ ፡ ዘንድ ፡ ወደ ፡ ከተማው ፡ ሄደ ። ዮሴፍም ፡ ደግሞ ፡ ከዳዊት ፡ ቤትና ፡ ወገን ፡ ስለ ፡ ነበረ ፡ ከገሊላ ፡ ከናዝሬት ፡ ከተማ ፡ ተነሥቶ ፡ ቤተ ፡ ልሔም ፡ ወደምትባል ፡ ወደ ፡ ዳዊት ፡ ከተማ ፡ ወደ ፡ ይሁዳ ÷ ፀነሰ ፡ ከነበረች ፡ ከእጮኛው ፡ ከማርያም ፡ ጋር ፡ ይጻፍ ፡ ዘንድ ፡ ወጣ ። በዚ ያም ፡ ሳሉ ፡ የመውለጃዋ ፡ ወራት ፡ ደረሰ ÷ የበ ኩር ፡ ልጅዋንም ፡ ወለደች ÷ በመጠቅለያም ፡ ጠቀለለችው ፤ በእንግዶችም ፡ ማደሪያ ፡ ስፍራ ፡ ስላልነበራቸው ፡ በግርግም ፡ አስተኛችው ።

ብስራተ፡ገብርኤል፡

ወዘቀፈ፡እሰላ፡ተ

8

$\mathcal{A}$nd there were in the same country shepherds living out in the fields, keeping watch over their flock by night. And behold, an angel of the Lord stood before them, and the glory of the Lord shone around them, and they were greatly afraid.

And the angel said to them, "Do not be afraid, for behold, I bring you good tidings of great joy which will be to all people. For there is born to you this day in the city of David a Savior, who is Christ the Lord. And this will be the sign to you: You will find a babe wrapped in swaddling cloths, lying in a manger."

And suddenly there was with the angel a multitude of the heavenly host praising God and saying:

"Glory to God in the highest,
And on earth peace,
    good will toward men!"

And so it was, when the angels had gone away from them into heaven, that the shepherds said to one another, "Let us now go to Bethlehem and see this thing that has come to pass, which the Lord has made known to us."

And they came with haste and found Mary and Joseph, and the babe lying in a manger. And when they had seen it, they made widely known the saying which was told them concerning this child. And all those who heard it marveled at those things which were told them by the shepherds. But Mary kept all these things and pondered them in her heart. And the shepherds returned, glorifying and praising God for all the things that they had heard and seen, as it was told to them.

በዚያም ፡ ምድር ፡ መንጋቻውን ፡ በሌሊት ፡ ሲጠብቁ ፡ በሜዳ ፡ ያደሩ ፡ እረኞች ፡ ነበሩ ። እንዘዎም ÷ የጌታ ፡ መልአክ ፡ ወደ ፡ እነሱ ፡ ቀረብ ፡ የጌታ ፡ ክብርም ፡ በዙሪያቸው ፡ አበራ ÷ ታላቅ ፡ ፍርሀትም ፡ ፈሩ ። መልአኩም ፡ እንዲህ ፡ አላቸው ፡ — እነሆ ÷ ለሕዝቡ ፡ ሁሉ ፡ የሚሆን ፡ ታላቅ ፡ ደስታ ፡ የምሥራች ፡ እነግራችኋለሁና ፡ አትፍሩ ፤ ዛሬ ፡ በዳዊት ፡ ከተማ ፡ መድኃኒት ፡ እርሱም ፡ ክርስቶስ ፡ ጌታ ፡ የሆነ ፡ ተወልዶላችኋል ። ይሀም ፡ ምልክት ፡ ይሆንላችኋል ፡ ሕፃን ፡ ተጠቅልሎ ፡ በግርግምም ፡ ተኝቶ ፡ ታገኛላችሁ ። ድንገትም ፡ ብዙ ፡ የሰማይ ፡ ሠራዊት ፡ ከመል አክ ፡ ጋር ፡ ነበሩ ። እግዚአብሔርንም ፡ እያመሰገኑ ፡ — ክብር ፡ ለእግዚአብሔር ፡ በአርያም ፡ ይሁን ፡ ሰላምም ፡ በምድር ፡ ለሰዎም ፡ በጎ ፡ ፈቃድ ፡ አለ ።

መላእክትም ፡ ከእነርሱ ፡ ተለይተው ፡ ወደ ፡ ሰማይ ፡ በወጡ ፡ ጊዜ ÷ እረኞቹ ፡ እርስ ፡ በር ሳቸው ፡ — እንግዲህ ፡ እስከ ፡ ቤተ ፡ ልሔም ፡ ድረስ ፡ እንሂድ ፡ እግዚአብሔርም ፡ የገለጠለ ንን ፡ ይሀን ፡ የሆነውን ፡ ነገር ፡ እንይ ፡ ተባባሉ ። ፈጥነውም ፡ መጡ ፡ ማርያምንና ፡ ዮሴፍን ፡ ሕፃ ኑንም ፡ በግርግም ፡ ተኝቶ ፡ አገኙ ። አይተ ውም ፡ ስለዚህ ፡ ሕፃን ፡ የተነገረላቸውን ፡ ነገር ፡ ገለጡ ። የሰሙትም ፡ ሁሉ ፡ እረኞቹ ፡ በነገሩ ፡ አቸው ፡ ነገር ፡ አደነቁ ፤ ማርያም ፡ ግን ፡ ይሀን ፡ ነገር ፡ ሁሉ ፡ በልብዋ ፡ እያሰበች ፡ ትጠብቀው ፡ ነበር ። እረኞችም ፡ እንደ ፡ ተባለላቸው ፡ ስለ ፡ ሰሙትና ፡ ስላዩት ፡ ሁሉ ፡ እግዚአብሔርን ፡ እያ መሰገኑና ፡ እያከበሩ ፡ ተመለሱ ።

ሊገርዞት ፡ ስምንት ፡ ቀን ፡ በሞላ ፡ ጊዜ ÷ በማ ኅፀን ፡ ሳይረገዝ ፡ በመልአኩ ፡ እንደ ፡ ተባለ ÷ ስሙ ፡ ኢየሱስ ፡ ተብሎ ፡ ተጠራ ።

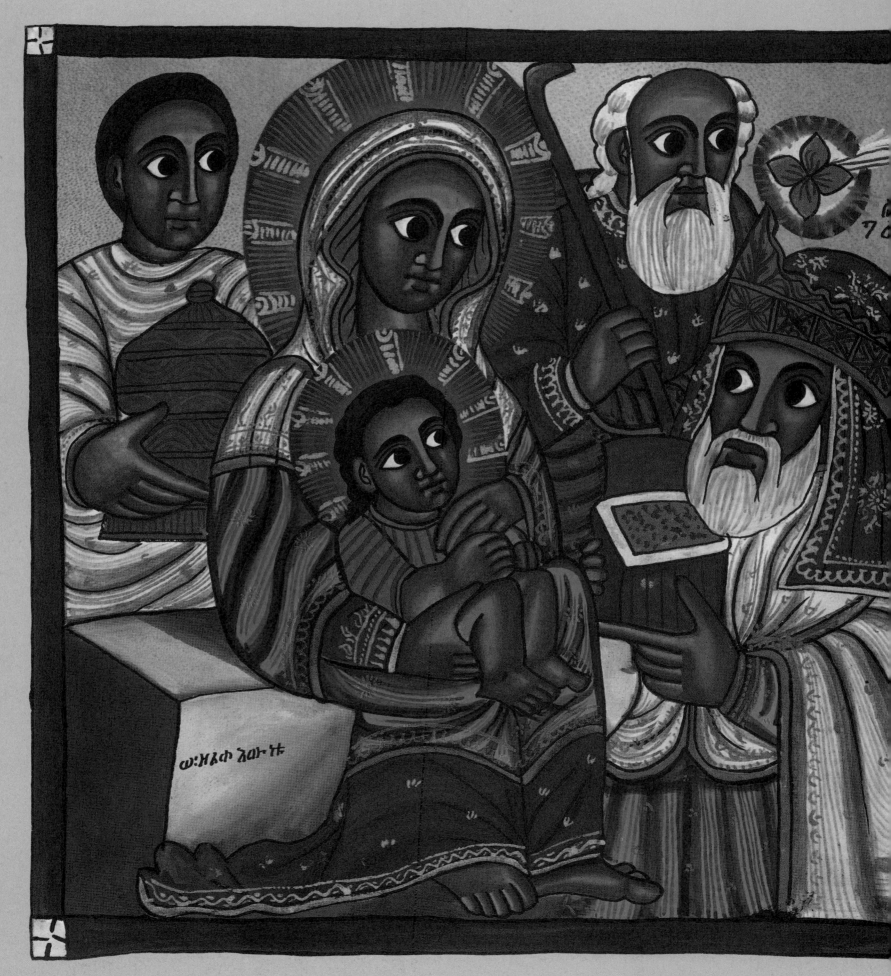

ወ፡ዘፈቅ እባኍ ኍ

10

Now after Jesus was born in Bethlehem of Judea in the days of Herod the king, behold, wise men from the East came to Jerusalem, saying, "Where is he who has been born King of the Jews? For we have seen his star in the East and have come to worship him."

When Herod the king had heard these things, he was troubled, and all Jerusalem with him. And when he had gathered all the chief priests and scribes of the people together, he inquired of them where the Christ was to be born.

And they said to him, "In Bethlehem of Judea, for thus it is written by the prophet:

'And you, Bethlehem, in the
    land of Judah,
Are not the least among
    the rulers of Judah;
For out of you will come a Ruler
Who will shepherd my people
    Israel.' "

Then Herod, when he had secretly called the wise men, determined from them what time the star appeared. And he sent them to Bethlehem and said, "Go and search diligently for the young child, and when you have found him, bring back word to me, that I may come and worship him also."

When they had heard the king, they departed; and behold, the star which they had seen in the East went before them, till it came and stood over where the young child was. When they saw the star, they rejoiced with exceedingly great joy.

And when they had come into the house, they saw the young child with Mary his mother, and fell down and worshiped him. And when they had opened their treasures, they presented gifts to him: gold, frankincense, and myrrh.

And being warned by God in a dream that they should not return to Herod, they departed for their own country another way.

ኢየሱስም ፡ በይሁዳ ፡ ቤተ ፡ ልሔም ፡ በን
ጉሡ ፡ በሄሮድስ ፡ ዘመን ፡ በተወለደ ፡ ጊዜ ፡
እነሆ ፡ ሰብአ ፡ ሰገል ፡— የተወለደው ፡ የአይ
ሁድ ፡ ንጉሥ ፡ ወዴት ፡ ነው ? ክከቡን ፡ በምሥ
ራቅ ፡ አይተን ፡ ልንስግድለት ፡ መጥተናልና ፡
እያሉ ፡ ከምሥራቅ ፡ ወደ ፡ ኢየሩሳሌም ፡ መጡ ፡
ንጉሡ ፡ ሄሮድስም ፡ ሰምቶ ፡ ደነገጠ ÷ ኢየሩሳ
ሌምም ፡ ሁሉ ፡ ከእርሱ ፡ ጋር ፡ የካህናትንም ፡
አለቆች ፡ የሕዝቡንም ፡ ጸሐፍት ፡ ሁሉ ፡ ሰብስቦ ፡
ክርስቶስ ፡ ወዴት ፡ እንዲወለድ ፡ ጠየቃቸው ።
እነርሱም ፡—

እንጂ ፡ ቤተ ፡ ልሔም ፡ የይሁዳ ፡ ምድር፡
ከይሁዳ ፡ ገዢዎች ፡ ከቶ ፡ አታንሽም ፡ ሕዝ
ቤን ፡ እስራኤልን ፡ የሚጠብቅ ፡ መስፍን ፡
ከአንቺ ፡ ይወጣልና ፡
ተብሎ ፡ በነቢይ ፡ እንዲህ ፡ ተጽፎአልና ፡ በይ
ሁዳ ፡ ቤተ ፡ ልሔ ፡ ም ፡ ነው ፡ አሉት ።

ከዚህ ፡ በኋላ ፡ ሄሮድስ ፡ ሰብአ ፡ ሰገልን ፡ በስ
ውር ፡ ጠርቶ ፡ ከከቡ ፡ የታየባትን ፡ ዘመን ፡
ከእነርሱ ፡ በጥንቃቄ ፡ ተረዳ ÷ ወደ ፡ ቤተ ፡
ልሔምም ፡ እነርሱን ፡ ሰድዶ ፡— ሂዱ ÷ ስለ ፡
ሕፃኑ ፡ በጥንቃቄ ፡ መርምሩ ፡ ባገኛችሁትም ፡
ጊዜ ፡ እኔ ፡ ደግሞ ፡ መጥቼ ፡ እንድሰግድለት ፡
ንገሩኝ ፡ አላቸው ፡ እነርሱም ፡ ንጉሡን ፡ ሰም
ተው ፡ ሄዱ ÷ በምሥራቅ ፡ ያዩት ፡
ክከብ ፡ ሕፃኑ ፡ ባለበት ፡ ላይ ፡ መጥቶ ፡ እስኪ
ቆም ፡ ድረስ ፡ ይመራቸው ፡ ነበር ። ክከቡንም ፡
ባዩ ፡ ጊዜ ፡ በታላቅ ፡ ደስታ ፡ እጅግ ፡ ደስ ፡ አላ
ቸው ÷ ወደ ፡ ቤትም ፡ ገብተው ፡ ሕፃኑን ፡ ከእ
ናቱ ፡ ከማርያም ፡ ጋር ፡ አዩት ÷ ወድቀውም ፡
ሰገዱለት ÷ ሣጥኖቻቸውንም ፡ ከፍተው ፡ እጅ
መንሻ ፡ ወርቅና ፡ ዕጣን ፡ ከርቤ ፡ አቀረቡለት ÷
ወደ ፡ ሄሮድስም ፡ እንዳይመለሱ ፡ በሕልም ፡ ተረ
ድተው ፡ በሌላ ፡ መንገድ ፡ ወደ ፡ አገራቸው ፡ ሄዱ ።

And when they had departed, behold, an angel of the Lord appeared to Joseph in a dream, saying, "Arise, take the young child and his mother, flee to Egypt, and stay there until I bring you word; for Herod will seek the young child to destroy him."

When he arose, he took the young child and his mother by night and departed into Egypt, and was there until the death of Herod, that it might be fulfilled which was spoken by the Lord through the prophet, saying, "Out of Egypt I have called my Son."

እንርሱም ፡ ከሄዱ ፡ በኋላ ፡ እነሆ ÷ የጌታ ፡ መልአክ ፡ በሕልም ፡ ለዮሴፍ ፡ ታየዉ ÷ ሄሮድስ ፡ ሕፃኑን ፡ ሊገድለዉ ፡ ይፈልገዋልና ፡ ተነሣ ÷ ሕፃኑንና ፡ እናቱንም ፡ ይዘህ ፡ ወደ ፡ ግብፅ ፡ ሽሽ ÷ እስክነግርህም ፡ ድረስ ፡ በዚያ ፡ ተቀመጥ ፡ አለዉ ።

እርሱም ፡ ተነሥቶ ፡ ሕፃኑንና ፡ እናቱን ፡ በሌሊት ፡ ያዘና ፡ ከጌታ ፡ ዘንድ ፡ በነቢይ ፡ — ልጄን ፡ ከግብፅ ፡ ጠራሁት ፡ የተባለዉ ፡ እንዲፈጸም ፡ ወደ ፡ ግብፅ ፡ ሄደ ÷ ሄሮድስም ፡ እስኪሞት ፡ ድረስ ፡ በዚያ ፡ ኖረ ።

የማርያም፡ሰደተ፡

ወ፡ዘእቀ፡እሎ፡ዛዚ

13

William Booth

1829-1912

HENRY GARIEPY

William Booth, God's soldier, could little realize when he embarked on his ministry to the poor that he would become the founder of a worldwide movement and take a place among the great Christian leaders of history. Seventy-five years after Booth's death, the sun never sets on The Salvation Army flag; it encircles the globe in 90 countries and territories.

Poverty and suffering were rampant in East London in 1865. Churches were often closed to the poor who were dirty, poorly clothed, and therefore not accepted. Booth, resolving to bring God's love to the poor, took the gospel to them in the open-air. He said, "Go for souls and go for the worst, netting the very sewers."

With his wife, Catherine, William Booth felt called to minister to the poor and destitute in London's East End and started in 1865 what was first called The Christian Mission. The name was changed in 1878 to The Salvation Army. Booth and his followers evangelized and applied practical measures of Christianity to such issues as child labor, slum housing, alcoholism, disease, and crime. Feeding stations were opened, shelters provided, employment programs launched, and a host of programs started—all precursors of the extensive ministries of the Army today.

All of Booth's ministry and social services were based on his love for God, his belief in salvation and God's Word, and his full commitment to Jesus Christ. His life motto was, "Others." On one occasion he wrote, "Some men's passion is fame; some men's passion is wealth; some men's passion is pleasure; my passion is souls." The secret of his life was, he stated, "As a young man I gave my all to Jesus Christ, and I never took it back."

The distinctives of the movement he founded have remained to the present day, including its paramilitary structure, equality of women, social services as an expression of its beliefs, internationalism, and fundamental Christian doctrines and practice, including total abstinence from alcohol and tobacco.

The Salvation Army, again this Christmas season, will follow the mandate of its founder, who in his last public address, declared:

While women weep as they do now,
  I'll fight!
While little children go hungry as they do now,
  I'll fight!
While men go to prison, in and out, in and out,
  I'll fight!
While there yet remains one dark soul without the light of God,
  I'll fight—I'll fight to the very end!

A Time for Giving

HENRY GARIEPY

In nearly every city and town The Salvation Army volunteer with the red kettle is a tradition of the Christmas season. The devotion to Jesus Christ of the one and a half million world membership results in a joyful commemoration for the world's greatest gift at Christmas: "God so loved the world that he gave his only Son" (John 3:16). Salvationists believe the coming of Christ into the world, which we celebrate at Christmas, is the most sublime and superlative gift to humankind. It is God's unspeakable gift to us of love, salvation, abundant and eternal life.

Such an incomparable gift from God motivates those who form The Salvation Army to give and share with others. It is the world's biggest dispenser of gifts of love each Christmas, reaching over three million persons with its Christmas cheer programs.

Beyond the music and mistletoe, beyond the tinsel and toys, many people are silently hurting. There are many among the hungry, the homeless, the lonely, and the disadvantaged for whom Christmas would be just another day if it were not for the practical remembrances of The Salvation Army.

The Salvation Army provides groceries, clothing, and toys for needy families, shelter for the homeless, and hot meals and companionship for the elderly.

And The Salvation Army's work does not end when the holiday decorations are taken down. Disaster relief, day care, medical services, family counseling, and spiritual guidance are just a few of the many fine services offered year-round.

Many segments of society join forces with the Army, making it the most comprehensive charitable undertaking in the world. Rotarians, Kiwanians, women's auxiliaries and clubs, schools, the Marines, youth groups, celebrities, professional athletes, the media, and a host of individuals help to make up the over one-million volunteer task force at Christmastime.

Famous personalities who have provided leadership and contributed their talents to the Christmas program have included Bill Cosby, Pat Boone, Robert Young, Betsy Palmer, the late Colonel Harland Sanders, and Bob Hope.

The following message from Bob Hope appeared as an advertisement the year he served as Christmas chairman: "I've travelled the globe entertaining U.S. troops in need of a boost in morale. And wherever I go I see The Salvation Army at work, offering spiritual guidance, material

(below left) The familiar red kettle beckons Christmas shoppers to remember the needy. The money raised funds a year-round ministry. (right) So that no child is forgotten, volunteers dress thousands of dolls to be given away at Christmas.

15

assistance, compassion and understanding to the world's people.

"This special brand of Christian outreach can also be found close to home. The Salvation Army operates day care and corps community centers, rehabilitation programs, clubs for senior citizens, recreation for all age groups, and emergency disaster services, to name just a few of its year-round activities."

Yes, the famous, but also the not-so-famous, are an essential part of the Army's Christmas team. Thousands of "unknowns" are moved yearly to contribute to the Army's Christmas kettle. It takes everyone—young and old, rich and poor—many hands and hearts to help reach the less fortunate.

Doll trees have become a trademark of the Salvation Army Christmas programs. Across the nation women auxiliary members and volunteers gather and dress dolls to give to children at Christmas. Thousands of dolls are beautifully dressed, each one destined to bring a smile to a child at Christmas. The Salvation Army invites everyone to share in bringing happiness to others at Christmas. Even the Marines have joined forces with The Salvation Army in their Toys for Tots program.

The business of The Salvation Army is to see that no one is forgotten at Christmas. It reaches out to the lonely, to the institutionalized, to those in prison and in nursing homes, to children and families in need.

The following poem, entitled "The Child Without a Christmas," expresses the importance to a child of being remembered at Christmastime.

> When all the world is silent
> on this holiest of nights,
> in a million beds the small ones dream
> of Christmasy delights.
> But some awaken sadly
> and their tiny hearts are numb
> when they realize through tear-filled eyes
> that Santa didn't come.
> A bit of cold or hunger
> are things they understand.
> But a Christmas without toys
> to hold in heart and hand
> means that someone has forgotten,
> that someone didn't care,
> that someone failed to listen
> to a very special prayer.
> It's, oh, so very hard to tell
> a disappointed tot
> just why she had to be the one
> that Santa Claus forgot.

Volunteers stand at the Christmas kettles, sometimes in frigid climate, to raise monies to get the job done. The familiar red kettle on the streets and in the shopping malls at Christmastime is the means by which millions share with others at Christmas.

The kettle itself has an interesting history. In 1891, The Salvation Army captain in San Francisco resolved to provide a free Christmas dinner to the area's poor persons. But how would he pay for the food?

As he went about his daily tasks, the question stayed in his mind. Suddenly, his thoughts went back to his days as a sailor in Liverpool, England. On the Stage Landing he had seen a large pot, called "Simpson's pot,"

into which charitable donations were thrown by passersby.

The very next morning, he secured permission from the authorities to place a similar pot at the Oakland ferry landing, at the foot of Market Street. No time was lost in securing the pot and placing it in a conspicuous position, so that it could be seen by all those going to and from the ferry boats. In addition, a brass urn was placed on a stand in the waiting room for the same purpose.

Thus, Captain Joseph McFee launched a tradition that has spread not only throughout the United States but throughout the world.

By Christmas 1895, the kettle was used in 30 Salvation Army corps in various sections of the West Coast area. *The Sacramento Bee* of that year carried a description of the Army's Christmas activities and mentioned the contributions to street-corner kettles. Shortly afterward, two young Salvation Army officers who had been instrumental in the original use of the kettle, William A. McIntyre and N. J. Lewis, were transferred to the East. They took with them the idea of the Christmas kettle.

In 1897, McIntyre prepared his Christmas plans for Boston around the kettle, but his fellow officers refused to cooperate for fear of "making spectacles of themselves." So McIntyre, his wife, and his sister set up three kettles at the Washington Street thoroughfare in the heart of the city. That year the kettle effort in Boston and other locations nationwide resulted in 150,000 Christmas dinners for the needy.

In 1898, the *New York World* hailed The Salvation Army kettles as "the newest and most novel device for collecting money." The newspaper also observed, "There is a man in charge to see that contributions are not stolen."

In 1901, kettle contributions in New York City pro-

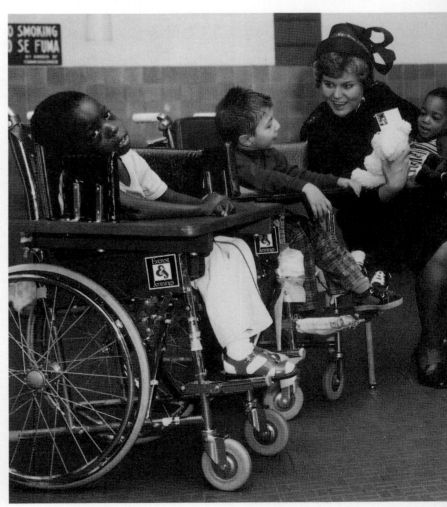

vided funds for the first mammoth sit-down dinner in Madison Square Garden, a custom that continued for many years. Today, however, families are given grocery checks so that they can buy and prepare their own dinners at home. The homeless poor, however, are still invited to share holiday dinners and festivities at hundreds of Salvation Army centers.

Kettles now are used in such distant lands as Korea, Japan, and Chile, and in many European countries.

(left) A member of The Salvation Army visits children in an institution. (below) One of the famous personalities to have helped with the Army's Christmas programs is comedian Bill Cosby. (bottom) The lonely and elderly are remembered.

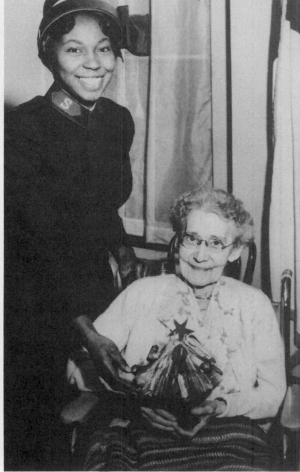

Everywhere, public contributions to the kettles enable The Salvation Army to bring the spirit of Christmas to those who would otherwise be forgotten—to the aged and lonely, the ill, the inmates of jails and other institutions, the poor and unfortunate. In the United States alone, The Salvation Army annually aids more than three million persons at Thanksgiving and Christmas.

Kettles have changed since the first utilitarian cauldron was set up in San Francisco. Some of the new kettles have such devices as a booth complete with a public address system over which the traditional Christmas carols are broadcast. Behind it all, though, is the same Salvation Army message, "Sharing Is Caring."

The modern Salvationist at the kettle will, no doubt, be dressed in the contemporary uniform that has replaced the traditional Army bonnet. But the motivation and mission is still the same—to bring the joy of Christmas to others in the name and spirit of the Lord Jesus, who came into the world that first Christmas.

Its Christmas cheer ministry takes many forms and goes beyond many walls and places of need. The lonely, the shut-in, the ill, are all part of the Army's parish at Christmas. But The Salvation Army not only provides bread for the body at Christmas, it offers bread for the soul as well. It recognizes that the spiritual hunger of people is often more acute than their material hunger. Advent worship, concerts, and outreach programs are conducted by its centers and institutions.

The true meaning and message of Christmas is highlighted. The Salvation Army believes and emphasizes that "Jesus is the reason for the season." It looks beyond the gifts to the Giver, beyond the friends to the Friend, beyond the lights to the Light, beyond the loneliness to the Lover, beyond the agonies to the Answer, beyond the pain to the One who came to bring peace.

Its major spiritual proclamation is made through the Christmas edition of *War Cry*, a publication colossus of over 4.8 million copies. This 24-page magazine is fully devoted to the Advent message as found in the good news of the Bible and incarnated in Christian experience. The special Christmas edition reaches a pluralistic parish that includes businesses, homes, institutions, hospitals, prisons, colleges, seminaries, inner cities, and the general public, many who receive their copy as they make their contribution at the Christmas kettle. Its circulation is without peer in the world of Christmas publications and represents the commitment of the organization to maintain the primacy of the spiritual in its extraordinary Christmas endeavors.

The *War Cry* features not only articles by its own writers from The Salvation Army, but in recent years has included such well-known contributors as Charles Swindoll, Marjorie Holmes, Joni Eareckson Tada, Billy Graham, and Charles Colson.

Soldiers and stalwarts of this army of God are dedicated to making the greatest story ever told a reality in the hearts and lives of others. At Christmastime, especially, untold numbers swell the ranks of this great army with generous contributions to the inescapable red kettle. Through practical expressions of help and through the proclamation of the gospel message the Savior is revealed to the nations. For The Salvation Army, Christmas is a time for giving and, most of all, for sharing the world's greatest love story.

A Sunny Christmas

ELSIE PHILLIPS

The Phillips had moved East near the end of September. Eager to get acquainted, they had immediately transferred their membership to a large church, which they attended regularly.

As Alan casually turned over the bulletin in church on the first Sunday in December, he saw this notice:

> WANTED—Some folks to play mother and dad to a little crippled boy in one of our hospitals who has never been in a home at Christmas.

Alan nudged Elsie, and she read it. From then on she found it hard to concentrate on the sermon. On the way home, Alan asked, "Do you suppose you could dig out that old Santa suit you made?"

Elsie answered that she had intended to find it before the Allisons came. "I think it is packed with the ornaments." Ted and May Allison were college friends who were driving 50 miles and bringing their two children to visit the Phillips for Christmas.

Alan said, "Since we are putting up a tree, why not invite the little fellow from the hospital for Christmas Day too. He would be about Buddy Allison's age." So it was decided.

While Elsie was getting dinner, she overheard Alan's part of the telephone conversation: "We saw your notice in our church bulletin, and we'd like to take that little

chap for Christmas. We took two little tykes two years ago and had lots of fun doing it."

There was a long pause, then Alan continued, "No, no, we have no children, but we have guests coming with their two. And my wife used to be a kindergarten teacher, so she knows how to entertain youngsters." The person at the other end did a lot of talking. Then Alan added definitely, "Oh, no, no, we wouldn't think of adopting any. I thought your notice said, 'To have Christmas Day in a home.'"

Alan paused for another long explanation and then asked, "How old is the lad? Uh, huh. Too bad. How sad. Tough luck." Again Alan paused, "Oh, no, we wouldn't consider anything except Christmas, or, if you want, the holiday week. I'll send in the references, and you'll let us know? Okay. Good-bye."

The Phillips' references were acceptable. So, as arranged, at four o'clock on December 23 Elsie stopped at the hospital and walked up the steps to the big, institutional doors. A stocky boy about four years old stood inside, his nose flattened against the glass. He tugged to open the door. "Hello. I've been waiting for you for a long time," he said.

Elsie stopped, "For me?" She started to ask why, but checked herself. She had pictured a little crippled boy, and this fellow was husky.

"The nurse told me you were coming this afternoon, so I've been watching for you. Say, am I going to ride in that shiny blue car? I'll get my coat; you wait right here. Here's Pluto." His brace clicked on the tile floor as he hustled down the long corridor. Elsie found herself standing alone just inside the door, holding a blue plush dog, rather worn and staring at her with one glass eye.

A white capped, grey-haired nurse rose from the appointment desk in an alcove at the left. As she came forward, she was smiling kindly. "Do come in," she said. "I've been watching Sunny. S-u-n-n-y is the way we spell it. That's his nickname here. He hasn't said a word to anyone who has come in that door since lunch. But he acted like he knew you. And when he saw you sitting in the car, he said, 'Here she is! Can I go and meet her?' But I told him to wait. By the way, you are Mrs. Phillips, aren't you?" Elsie nodded.

"It's most unusual. You see, Dr. Brown told Sunny that some friends were coming to take him to their home for Christmas Day. But Sunny told the other children at lunch that his mom and dad were coming. He couldn't be persuaded to take his nap; he stuck right there at the door all afternoon. His parents are both dead, you know. He came here when he was still a baby, so this is the only home he knows. He's been with us three years. He had polio, but we hope in time he may have the brace off."

The little fellow returned that minute, so the conversation was cut short. His arms overflowed with coat, cap, and overshoes. Mittens fastened on a string dragged behind.

"So you want to go home with me for Christmas, do you?" Elsie asked.

Dumping the clothes on the floor, standing straight and as tall as his four years allowed, he looked at Elsie appraisingly. Then Elsie heard him ask, "Do you have a nice daddy at home?"

"Yes," she replied.

"Is he an awful, awful, awful nice daddy?" Sunny demanded.

"I think he is very nice."

"Well, then I want to go. I've been waiting for you for a long time."

Elsie seemed to be having difficulty with the coat buttons as she bent her head lower over the fastenings. There was a long silence; the nurse blew her nose hard and walked over to a clothes closet.

"This overshoe goes on my little leg," Sunny explained. "We can't hook it over my brace at the bottom, but I can hook the top. I'll show you." Then, for the first time, Elsie noticed "the little leg" as he tugged and pulled at the overshoe to buckle it at the top.

"The clothes he will need are in this little suitcase," the nurse said as she returned, her eyes glistening. "Oh, Sunny, I see you are taking Pluto, too. Well, okay, take him with you. Now give me a big hug and have lots of fun."

On the way home Sunny sat close to Elsie, stroking the fur on her sleeve or holding Pluto up so the plush dog could see out. He chattered freely about the gadgets on the dashboard of the car, but was especially intrigued by the windshield wipers, for now it was snowing. When they arrived at the duplex, he would not let Elsie out of his sight a second. Finally, she put a stool beside the sink so he could watch her make dinner.

That's where Alan found them. He kissed Elsie and then, chucking the lad under the chin, said, "I'm hungry enough to eat a horse. How about you?"

"This is Sunny, and this is Pluto, and they have come for Christmas," Elsie said by way of introduction.

"That's just great!" Alan responded. "I certainly will need a helper tomorrow to get the Christmas tree up. But now, if dinner is ready, let's get up to the table."

Sunny cleaned his plate quickly and then watched Alan, saying nothing. The grownups seemed to have difficulty keeping up a general conversation. When dessert was finished, Alan pushed his chair from the table and asked, "Now that we have some time before bedtime, what shall we play?"

A bit unenthusiastically, the four-year-old replied, "Well I 'spose we better play 'taking-out-tonsils.'" He stretched himself out on the couch, opened his mouth, shut his eyes, and lay still.

It took Alan a minute to get the idea that his patient was waiting. "Oh, dear, let's think of something else. I don't think I know how to play doctor," Alan said. "I tell you what. Come here and sit on my lap in this big chair

and tell me about . . . about," again he hesitated, "all about the hospital."

The boy picked up Pluto and sat on Alan's knee. But he said nothing.

"All right, Sunny, now tell me what you do there," Alan coaxed.

"There's nothing to tell."

"Can't you think of anything?"

"Nothin' 'cept spinach and operations."

"But what do you do there?"

"Nothing. I was just waiting."

"Waiting for what?"

"Just waiting for you and mommy."

Sparks popped from the fireplace. The boy and man brushed the red cinders back into the fire, watching intently and quietly as the fire burned more brightly. The child was drowsy; he had had no nap that day. Alan glanced at the brace fastened to the shoe and buckled with straps around the knee. Finally, the little fellow said, "I'd like a really, truly story about Christmas; a really, truly one."

*T*he dishes done, Elsie slipped in and sat down on a low stool. She brought pajamas from Sunny's suitcase and held them up to the fire to warm them. Alan began slowly, as though he were thinking up words as he talked. "A long, long time ago, there was a man whose name was Joseph, and his wife's name was Mary. They had to make a trip to a town a long way off. They had only one small donkey, so Mary rode it and Joseph walked beside her all the way. They were very tired when, that evening, they came to a small town. They went to the hotel, but the man who kept the hotel said . . ."

Sunny interrupted, "He said, 'There's no room for you at the inn.'"

"That's right." Alan continued, "'But,' he said, 'over in the barn you may make a bed on the sweet-smelling hay.' So they did. In the night a baby boy was born to Mary, and she was very happy. After that she felt better, and she and the baby slept on the hay."

"That was baby Jesus, wasn't it?" Sunny asked.

"Yes, it was." Slowly, as though seeking simple words, Alan went on. "Joseph saw that it seemed to be getting light outside, so he went out and looked, and there in the sky was the most beautiful star he had ever seen. It was so bright it made the night sky light. He went in and told Mary about it."

"And he told her about the angels didn't he," Sunny interjected, "and they were singing, weren't they?"

"That's right. It's a really, truly Christmas story, and tomorrow is Christmas Eve. Now off to bed, tired little boy, because tomorrow we must fix the Christmas tree, and there are lots of things to do. I'll need a big helper like you."

"Your pajamas are all nice and warm," said Elsie as she helped the sleepy child get dressed for bed.

She had borrowed a white iron youth bed and set it up in the guest room. But when she started to turn down the covers, Sunny ran out of the room, sobbing as though his heart was broken. Between sobs, they heard him say, "It's just like my hospital bed, and I thought I was going to sleep at home." No coaxing would get him near the bed until Alan suggested moving it into their bedroom, putting it right between their beds. Even then, not until they showed him that they would be sleeping right beside him would he crawl between the clean sheets. "Now I won't be lonesome anymore, mommy." Smiles lightened his tears as Elsie crawled into her bed.

Right after breakfast the next morning, Alan and Sunny went off to a tree lot. They found a nice tree and brought it home tied to the side of the car. Then Alan borrowed a neighbor boy's sled and hauled Sunny to the grocery store where they bought a big list of groceries for Elsie. With everything packed in a carton, Sunny proudly hauled the sled back.

They got home just in time to watch Elsie stuff the

turkey, something the lad had never seen before. In fact, until then he thought turkeys grew up already stuffed.

Then it was time for Alan and Sunny to string the lights and trim the tree before their guests arrived. Elsie was busy in the kitchen, but she came in frequently to offer her helpers a taste of the food she was preparing or to admire their efforts with the tree and house decorations. Sunny certainly was living up to his name. Everything was a thrill for him.

At about five o'clock the Allisons arrived, loaded with suitcases, extra blankets, packages, pies, and a new puppy. Sunny helped pull off overshoes and carried packages to the kitchen. He was absolutely unaware of the clicking sound his brace made and how the children stared at his little leg. When Ted Allison looked quizzically at the Phillips, Alan replied, "We took him from the hospital just to give him a nice Christmas."

From the moment the Allisons arrived, fun and laughter swept through the house. The children added ornaments they had brought along to the tree. Then after supper they hung their stockings, with their names printed in white, on the mantel. Elsie found a blue skating sock on which she pinned Christmas bells, and Sunny hung it up on the fireplace mantel with the others.

After the children were tucked in bed, Ted unlocked the trunk of the car and unloaded a gunny sack stuffed with packages. The Phillips added a pair of skates and a little football they had bought for the Allison children. Alan came up from the basement with his arms full of presents.

The next day it seemed as though the clock whirled around. Sunny entered into everything in high spirits, except that he would not play outside with the boys unless Alan was there too.

The Phillips did not have a minute to themselves. Secretly, they were avoiding time alone together. And, it seemed, the Allisons were in no hurry to leave, so they lingered over the cold turkey supper. Afterwards, they found it no small job to collect all their belongings, new toys, gifts, and dishes of food. Sunny held the new puppy. As they were about to go, he handed the dog to Buddy and said, "Don't forget to bring Jigs with you next time you come, 'cause I like him."

At last the Allisons were gone. Sunny was in bed. Elsie and Alan straightened up the house. Then as they tiptoed into their bedroom, Alan put his arm around Elsie and said, "What a Christmas!" They stood silently, looking at the sleeping child. One arm was around Pluto; the other was stretched out, clutching Alan's pillow. Neither spoke. Alan picked up the brace and looked at it for a long time. Finally he said determinedly, "I'm going to buy him a new bed tomorrow. Every boy needs a bed of his own."

Elsie threw herself into Alan's arms. "Oh, you darling, you darling! And Alan, I've thought of the loveliest name! Let's name him Noel, for he's the best Christmas gift we have ever had!" Both Elsie and Alan had tears in their eyes, tears of joy.

"We'll call the hospital first thing in the morning and tell them, 'Sunny is home to stay; he won't be back!' " Alan declared.

"And don't forget to tell the hospital folks we are naming him Noel, Christmas joy," laughed Elsie through her tears.

The Nativity

Rogier van der Weyden, 1399 or 1400-1464

ARTICLE BY PHILLIP GUGEL

This unusual version of the nativity by Northern Renaissance master painter Rogier van der Weyden is the main panel of a triptych done for Pierre Bladelin between 1452 and 1455. Used as an altarpiece or devotional picture, a triptych consists of one central panel with two hinged wings. The wings fold over the center panel and usually are painted on both sides. The *Bladelin Triptych* features three annunciation scenes—with Mary (exterior wings closed), with the Emperor Augustus (interior left wing), and with the Magi (interior right wing). These subjects complement the central panel nativity, which invites the viewer to contemplate Jesus' coming among us and to humbly adore him.

The naked infant in this nativity gazes at Mary while lying rather awkwardly on her skirts. In painting him this way, perhaps van der Weyden was emphasizing the helplessness, humanity, and poverty God donned in coming to our world. The carefully rendered features of the characters prove that the painter was not lacking in skill.

The centered position of Mary, aligned with the apex of the roof, is something rarely seen in depictions of the nativity. Her central position and the pencil-like rays of her halo denote the virgin's dominance among the figures arranged in a triangle around her son. Her prominence suggests that van der Weyden and his patron held Mary in high regard. Yet lost in adoration, she radiates humility and warmth.

Resplendent in red, Joseph presents an example of the novel symbolism van der Weyden favored in his paintings. Joseph shields his candle's artificial light so that the true light, embodied in the Christ child, may shine forth.

The inclusion of Pierre Bladelin, the patron of this work, as one of the three major figures who adore the holy infant is a daring and original innovation for a nativity painting. Pierre is drawn the same size as Joseph and Mary, making him equally important. Traditionally, ordinary humans were shown smaller than any holy persons with whom they appeared, as are the trios of angels pictured here. The fact that Pierre kneels with the holy family, rather than off to the side on one of the wings, indicates his importance. Also, of note, he comes by himself to adore, rather than with a patron saint. In traditional depictions of donors, a patron saint accompanies the donor.

This nativity painting fuses past and present time both by locating Jesus' coming in a Flemish landscape and by placing the donor within the holy family's sacred space. Though paradoxical, his approach imparts a reality to the birth, making it more than an announcement.

Most likely, Bladelin's inclusion in the nativity was done because he requested it. Patrons became increasingly important during the fifteenth century in Flanders (now the nation of Belgium). Donors from the rising middle class, such as Bladelin, were able to afford and to commission works from the best artists. Shedding their anonymity or timidity, their portraits were included in paintings of sacred events.

Rogier van der Weyden's positioning of the stable copies the unusual oblique angle used by the Master of Flémalle in his nativity (c. 1420). Van der Weyden, however, was the first painter to incorporate a large column into the ruin's architecture. Medieval legend claims that Mary used a column to support herself as she gave birth. An interplay of light and shadow pervades the interior of this Romanesque structure, whose stone masonry and thatched roof are convincingly rendered. The assorted plants growing from its foundation, walls, and roof are a botanist's delight, including several clumps of mushrooms that sprout from the thatched roof.

The structure's ruined foundation has two openings, possibly indicating there is a water cistern below. Scholars are uncertain as to what the artist was alluding in the foundation and cistern. Perhaps the former implies that the Old Testament synagogue is the New Testament church's foundation; the latter may allude to Bethlehem's well with its promise of salvation.

Besides lending a homely note to the nativity, the ox and ass have symbolic associations in medieval legend. The ox's attentive observation of Jesus' adoration signifies Christianity and its belief that Jesus is the Messiah. In contrast, only the nose of the ass is visible; its eyes are hidden, an indication in traditional iconography of Judaism's blindness to Jesus.

The Flemish landscape continues the juxtaposition of past and present time in the nativity. In the upper left corner, the angel's announcement to the shepherds is taking place. In the upper right corner, a delightful street scene of the Flemish town of Middelburg entices us.

Pierre Bladelin and his wife, Margaret, founded Middelburg as a town for poor and homeless people. Since they were childless, it was a way of utilizing their wealth for a beneficial and spectacular purpose. The construction of the town began in 1448 at a site north of Bruges, Belgium. This was the first time in about 400 years in northern Europe that such a venture was attempted.

Born in 1410 to a family of modest means, Pierre Bladelin advanced to become ambassador and tax collector for Philip the Good, Duke of Burgundy. Through his devoted and exemplary service he became influential, powerful and wealthy. When he died in 1472, his body was placed in a tomb at Middelburg's Church of Saints Peter and Paul. Upon her death, Margaret was placed in the same tomb. Originally, the *Bladelin Triptych* graced one of this church's altars.

Painted on a wooden panel measuring 35¾ inches by 35 inches, the nativity and its accompanying wings are in the collection of the Gemaldgalerie, Staatliche Museum, in Berlin-Dahlem, Germany.

Rogier van der Weyden was born at Tournai, Belgium. His accomplishments as a painter led the city council of Brussels (his wife Elizabeth's birthplace) to appoint him its official painter. Because he was held in such high regard, no one was chosen to succeed him in this post after his death. Van der Weyden's consummate skill as a painter was matched by his integrity and rare unselfishness. Probably no fifteenth century Flemish master, except for Jan van Eyck, exerted such an extensive influence on succeeding generations of painters as he did.

Van der Weyden's painting makes the mystery of the incarnation tangible to our senses, as well as to our minds. The naturalistic manner in which he depicted the birth of Christ was a way of enhancing its supernatural meaning. Perhaps no other Flemish painting concentrates on Jesus' birth as does the *Bladelin Triptych*. Captured by the visual impact of its nativity, we too can respond: "O come, let us adore him, Christ the Lord!"

The Messiah Strad

Antonio Stradivari, 1644-1737

CHARLES K. GRAY

The violinmaker sat in his workshop wearing a white leather apron. He had just applied the final coat of varnish to a violin that, from its beginning as blocks of pine, maple, and ebony, held a special place in his heart. He knew several weeks before that this would be one of his proudest creations. The process of this violin's birth passed before him as he held it up in the light.

He remembered the trips to northern Italy in search of the choicest pine, and the day when he had bought some of the finest marbled-grain maple he had ever seen from Venetian merchants. It had taken months to cut and carve this wood from solid blocks to the exact shape he wanted. He thought of the crucial cuts he had made with precision, as well as of those on other woodblocks that had been too deep, causing a work of inferior quality.

As he put the violin down on the workbench, the violinmaker thought of his countrymen—Vivaldi, Corelli, and Vitali, all famous violinists and composers—who had tested his talent with their performances and compositions. He wondered what they would think of his newest instrument, a violin without blemish.

His previous creations were sold to noblemen and worthy performers for about 30 dollars. Every violin had been sold, and he realized he had never desired to keep one for himself. No more, he thought, for he would hang this one on his wall as a monument to his cherished task, a symbol of perfection in his craft.

The year was 1716, and as Antonio Stradivari hung up his violin to dry, he had little time to admire the glow of its reddish-brown varnish. There were many orders waiting to be filled and he had just removed an instrument from that process. He needed to return to his one-man "assembly line" to complete his daily projects

and stay on schedule. His slow, meticulous work allowed him to complete only two instruments each month, but there were many more in various stages of production.

For the next 20 years the violin on the wall inspired Stradivari as nearly 350 more instruments were completed. While all of the instruments evidence his fine workmanship,

Stradivari's *Le Messie* is now part of the rare instrument collection of the Ashmolean Museum, Oxford.

none was to surpass that never-sold, never-played violin made in 1716. Antonio knew that this was a special violin, but he had no idea that 250 years later it would represent the pinnacle of violinmaking. Soon after his death in 1737 this violin became known as *Le Messie*, or "the Messiah," because of its unrivaled condition.

The fame of Antonio Stradivari is

known around the world. He is to violins what Rolls-Royce is to automobiles. Reports of record prices paid for his violins, most exceeding $500,000 today, are front-page news. What was involved in his violinmaking? Why do Stradivari instruments attract so much attention? And what has become of the violin called "the Messiah"?

In order to answer these questions it is appropriate to return to the time of the Italian Renaissance, more than 400 years ago. It was at this time in history that a new family of musical instruments, the strings—violin, viola, and cello—were born. Many designs were doubtless tried that are now forgotten. It was Andrea Amati, born about 1510, who created the design that is similar to today's familiar pattern. In 1538 Andrea Amati was able to lease, and later buy, the house in Cremona, Italy, which was to serve as the center of violinmaking for the next 200 years. It was in this house that succeeding generations of Amatis created many of the world's greatest instruments. And here the greatest of violinmakers, Antonio Stradivari, learned his trade.

The violin did not achieve immediate acceptance or wide popularity. Yet this changed slowly, and in 1560 Andrea Amati, then a well-established violinmaker, received an order for a large number of instruments. These were made for Charles IX of France, and are known as "the famous 24 violins of the king."

Antonio Stradivari was born in 1644 and began work in his early teens as a woodcarver. Shortly thereafter he became apprenticed to the violinmaker Nicolo Amati, grandson of Andrea. In 1666 he left Nicolo's shop and started work on his own. He lived to the age of 93, continuing to make instruments throughout his long life. Because he kept no day-to-day production records and many instruments would always be in various stages of production, the exact number of instruments that Stradivari made will never be known.

It was during Stradivari's lifetime that string instruments became the dominant instruments of western music. They were vital to chamber music, orchestral music, opera, and the music of the church. His instruments, although considered fine, were not as attractive to players and collectors as those of the Amati family. Consequently, many Stradivari works received careless treatment and were destroyed, badly damaged, or lost. About 700 Stradivari instruments can be authenticated as surviving today out of some 1200 that experts believe he made.

Today Stradivari violins are worth a fortune based on their art value alone. These instruments are objects of great speculation among collectors and dealers. Although few of these people are violinists they have something that most musicians do not, money. Collectors have been known to stare for hours at a violin that they intend to buy and never ask to hear it played.

Some violins have not been played in years. They sit in bank vaults or private collections, embedded in velvet and silk, the property of investors who are waiting for the most opportune time to make a profit. The price is rarely determined by the sound at all, but rather by the maker's fame and by the instrument's condition. However, the fact that many of the world's greatest violinists play on a Stradivarius owes itself not to the antique value but mainly to the sound of his violins.

The violin is made to be played. No instrument, with the possible exception of the human voice, provides such a vehicle for emotional expression. Few instruments compare with it in terms of musical versatility. The capacity for sustained sound, accent, and the variety of moods that are possible make the violin one of the most acoustically perfect instruments.

Composers, inspired by its potential, have written extensively for the violin as a solo instrument, accompanied and unaccompanied, and also in connection with the genres of orchestral and chamber music. Possibly no other instrument can boast a larger and musically more distinguished repertory, if one takes into account all forms of solo and ensemble music in which the violin has been assigned a part.

Sound quality is relative to the person who is listening. A trip to the neighborhood stereo store is proof enough that the same music heard through different equipment provides innumerable sound choices. With violins it is much the same, but the differences are less obvious to the untrained ear. In most cases, the average listener is not able to distinguish a Stradivarius from an excellent new violin. It has happened time and time again that in a comparison test the listener, believed to be listening to a Strad, was actually listening to a newer, less valuable instrument.

An incident involving the famous violinist Fritz Kreisler illustrates this point. Kreisler had recently purchased a Stradivarius and was playing it in public for the first time. The concert was held at Town Hall in New York City and the hall was overflowing with listeners anxious to be part of this historic event. The audience was certain that the legendary Kreisler would sound better than ever with this "new" instrument and they were not to be disappointed. As Kreisler played, those in attendance were awed by the aural beauty created as the bow moved across the strings. The crowd jumped to its feet as the last notes sounded before intermission.

After graciously bowing, Kreisler abruptly turned and smashed his violin on the piano bench. People were horrified at this sudden action and their mouths hung open in disbelief. Kreisler waited on stage for those in the audience to regain their composure. Then he spoke, "How easily you are fooled. This violin, which now lies in pieces, was purchased last week for 50 dollars! I will play my beautiful Stradivarius after intermission!"

Those in attendance that memorable day learned an important fact about violins and violinists. An average violinist makes a superior violin sound average; but a superior violinist can make an average violin sound like a Stradivarius.

What is it about a Stradivarius that makes it the preference of seasoned performers? This is a question that has puzzled players and stringed-instrument makers ever since the be-

The Making of a Violin

(above) Carrying on a tradition that began over 350 years ago, violinmaker Robert Black carefully shapes the back for a new violin. The pieces of wood selected for the violin are of utmost importance. Maple, chosen carefully for the beauty of the wood pattern, is used for the back, ribs, neck, and scroll. Spruce is used for the belly or front. The fingerboard, pegs, tailpiece, and nut are made of ebony or an ornamental rosewood or boxwood.

(below) To form the ribs or sides of an instrument, the maker begins with a wooden pattern, a template. Six spruce blocks, which will be used to reinforce the ribs, are carved to match the angles of the template and are lightly glued to its surface. Then thin maple strips are dampened, molded over a hot iron, and carefully fit over the wood blocks to give the ribs their graceful shape.

(bottom) The back is glued to the ribs, and a violin begins to take shape. Surfaces are planed to ensure an exact fit when the belly is added.

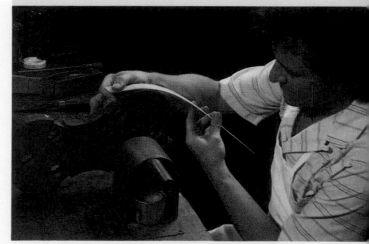

(above) The proportions of the violin, developed over centuries, vary little today. Each violinmaker still leaves a distinguishing characteristic in the crafting of the scroll, the f-holes, and the purfling, an ornamental inlay. Black puts his final imprint on a scroll he has cut from a rough block of wood.

(below) As well as providing a decorative border on both the front and back of the instrument, the purfling serves a useful purpose: if the violin is dropped, a crack that starts at the edge will be stopped at these three thin strips of wood. The strips are glued together and shaped over a hot iron. Next they are fitted into a narrow channel that has been cut along the edges of the front and back. The purfling is then trimmed level with the surface of the instrument.

(bottom) The f-holes, which allow sound to escape from the instrument, are carefully positioned on the belly. Though crooked f-holes will not affect the sound, they will flaw the appearance of the violin. The f-holes are traced onto the wood, using a template, and then cut out.

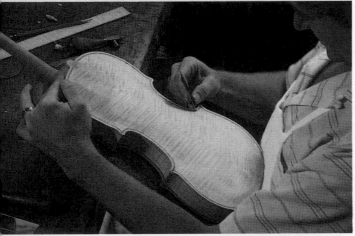

ginning of the nineteenth century. It was at this time that performers began to inquire of collectors and dealers to search out Stradivari instruments instead of Amatis, which were previously the favorites. They learned that the Strads could better withstand the increased string tension that was desired in the Romantic Period.

Precision instruments have been used to measure Stradivari violins. Using similar wood and measurements, Strad imitators build what they hope will be duplicates. Recent publications have appeared announcing a present-day maker as the next Stradivari. These statements pass quickly, for under scrutiny it becomes ever more obvious that, although these "duplicate" violins are excellent instruments, Stradivari remains unsurpassed. Good craftsmanship is not sufficient to attain a good tone. Precise workmanship and superior materials are no guarantee that a first-class soloist's violin is going to emerge.

Violin construction is much more difficult than it seems. A violin is made of about 70 different parts. There are usually three different woods used, pine or spruce for the top, maple for the back and sides, and ebony for the fingerboard, chinrest, tailpiece, and pegs. Rosewood and boxwood are sometimes substituted for ebony because of their decorative quality. The greatest difficulty in violinmaking lies in choosing the right piece of wood, making the correct cut, and then thinning the wood to achieve the proper ratio in thickness between the top and bottom pieces.

The wood begins in solid blocks and is cut and shaped closely following the pattern conceived by Andrea Amati. The grain of the top runs lengthwise, while the grain of the back most often runs side to side. In the sixteenth century it was determined that a violin sounded best when a soft wood was used for the top and a harder wood was used for the back and sides. Since the fingerboard was to be constantly under the pressure of the violinist's left hand, the dense wood, ebony, was selected in order to avoid the ruts that would quickly form in softer wood.

Once the top and back are finished the sides are shaped with water and

heat. Decorative sound holes are cut in the top before the box is glued together, using water soluble glue (in case the instrument ever needs to be opened up again for repair).

After the neck and peg box (scroll) have been added the violin is ready to be varnished. It is at this point that experts believe, either in formula or in method, Stradivari had a secret. His varnish is often discussed as the reason for his superior tonal results. Stradivari used an oil varnish, but the ingredients and application method are not known. The formula, reportedly kept in the family Bible, was lost before its importance was known.

If Stradivari had any secret in his varnishing method, it was the secret of infinite patience. For to make and apply pure oil varnish must be a labor of love. In one of his two surviving letters the master complains of the difficulty of getting the varnish to dry, adding, "Without the strong heat of the sun, the violin cannot reach the state of perfection." His descendants and ensuing generations would not wait for the agonizingly slow drying process of a pure oil varnish. They turned to alcohol-based varnishes for a much faster and more economical drying time.

Violin sounds are produced by the vibrations of the four strings, stretched tightly along the top of the violin from peg box to tailpiece. The strings are usually gut or perlon and are wound with silver or aluminum wire. Their combined tension reaches about 50 pounds, of which about 20 pounds is directed straight onto the bridge and against the sounding box. A small post of wood, called the soundpost, is inserted into the violin and wedged tightly between the top and bottom. This post serves to conduct the vibrations throughout and to keep the top of the violin from collapsing under the pressure of the string tension. As the bow passes over the strings, the friction causes vibrations, which are amplified in the box. The violin exhales and inhales, forcing vibrating air out of the sound holes.

The amount of pressure on the bow, and thus on the strings, controls the quality of sound that is produced. A parent of a young string student knows all too well how hard it is to produce a pure tone on the violin. Squeaks and scratches are the

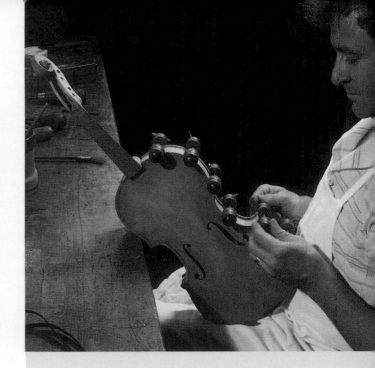

result when the bow pressure is not exact. It is the bow arm, just as much as the left hand, which constantly must be fine tuned in the playing of an excellent performer.

Most professional violinists dream of owning a Stradivarius. This dream is based not on financial gain, but on sound and playing ease. The subtle differences that appear insignificant to the average ear are of great importance to an artist. Most of those attending Kreisler's recital heard no difference between the 50-dollar violin and the Stradivarius. What Kreisler noticed was the range and dimension of the Stradivarius tone. He felt the difference in the power of the sound, carrying to the farthest corners of the concert hall. Speed of response and balance of sound mark important characteristics distinguishing a Strad from other instruments.

In order to achieve the "expected" results from a Strad, the player must be gifted, experienced, and patient. These great violins have the potential of infinite nuance and give the player the feeling of limitless depth in the sound. In order to get the most out of a Strad it may take more than a year of hard work and experimentation. After playing an "ordinary" instrument, a violinist must learn to use more bow speed and to apply less pressure in order to coax the singing soprano voice out of the violin. The well-known violinist Yehudi Menuhin states, "One must rise to a Strad before it will speak from its craftsman's soul. It is like a highly bred racehorse, capable of the greatest feats of endurance, of brilliance, of self-discipline and control, and yet so proud and unbending as never to allow itself to be ridden by anything less than the lightest, most flexible touch. It is perfection and must be played to perfection."

Stradivari did not have the benefit of today's sophisticated equipment, yet his instruments are preferred for tonal and artistic reasons. His success was due to materials, formulas, intuitive skill, and understanding, as well as to good timing. He had the greatest violinmaker of his time, Nicolo Amati, for a teacher. He worked slowly and carefully and made changes in his design at just the right moment to take advantage of later, unforeseen innovations in violin playing. He copied his teacher during his early years and later began to experiment with different cuts and measurements of wood. These experiments continued throughout the remainder of his life as Stradivari tried ceaselessly to produce ever greater instruments.

Broadly speaking, Stradivari profited by experience and, as he grew older, avoided the shortcomings noticeable in his earlier productions. Points of similarity with Amati became less and less as his art developed. He produced works of varying merit—some very successful and others failing somewhat, though he never made poor instruments; even his inferior violins stand out when compared to another violinmaker's best examples.

The year 1690 marked an important change in Stradivari's design as he developed a longer pattern for his violins. The instruments made during the years 1690-1698, when he used this shape, are known as "long Strads." After returning briefly to an Amati pattern, Stradivari began the period known as the "Golden Period," which lasted from 1700-1720. Violins produced during this period are among the most highly sought after due to their exceptional wood, varnish, proportion, and tone.

Stradivari continued to make fine violins even as he passed his eightieth and ninetieth birthdays. He was so proud of this fact that he recorded his age in several instruments made during his last ten years.

Stradivari rarely imitated himself, making it even more difficult to imitate him. Most of the instruments offered to museums and dealers today as "newly discovered Strads" turn out to be cheap, mass-produced, factory-made instruments, worth between 100 and 200 dollars. For 150 years European violinmakers have glued "Stradivarius labels" in their instruments, but usually just for show. There are an unlimited number of violins on the market today bearing the same label: "Antonius Stradivarius Cremonenfis Faciebat Anno ____," followed by the year, which may be anywhere from 1666-1737. Stradivarius is probably the most forged name in the world. Most often these labels are not meant to

(above) Weeks of painstaking work precede the assembly of an instrument. Front, back, and sides are carved, shaved, and scraped to proper thicknesses, gauged with a caliper to measure to the tenth of a millimeter. The bass bar and the soundpost, internal sound conductors, are carved and positioned. The body then is glued and held together with a series of clamps.

(below) Black applies a last coat of varnish to a completed violin. Many makers ascribe the unsurpassed sound of Stradivari's instruments to the ingredients of his varnish. A bad varnish can ruin a good violin, but a good varnish enhances both the sound and the appearance of an instrument. Varnishes are made from an endless variety of resins and can range in color from a tawny gold to a deep red.

(bottom) The soundpost is adjusted during the fine-tuning process to bring out the fullest sound of the violin. Other final adjustments are completed: the bridge is fitted and the strings are tuned to the proper pitches. The violin is then ready to be played.

deceive but, rather, to inform the owner what Stradivari violin has been copied.

Strangely enough, there has never been a law against bogus Strads. Some of the many stories about instruments bearing false Stradivari labels were collected in an article in the *Wall Street Journal* titled "If You Own a Stradivarius and Hate Bad News, Don't Read This Story." The article tells of a widow who came to Sotheby's auction house saying that her husband had left his sizable estate to other relatives, and to his beloved spouse only "the family Strad," since it was worth the most. Its worth? Two hundred dollars! Another story tells of a couple who never saved a penny, knowing that they could always cash in their "secret treasure" to bring them money for their retirement.

In the years following Stradivari's death other makers emerged. The names of Guadagnini, Gagliano, and Guarneri became better known than Stradivari. Although his son, Paolo, labored constantly to have his father remembered by the city of Cremona, Stradivari was all but forgotten by 1760. In fact, had it not been for the work of Luigi Tarisio, few if any of the marvelous Strads copied in past years would have survived. This mysterious man about whom little is known took on the task of saving the violins of old Cremona.

*T*arisio became interested in Stradivari violins because his violin teacher owned one. His teacher had mentioned repeatedly that he should go to Cremona and visit the cradle of violinmaking. "There are few of these beautiful violins left," he had told Luigi. "Perhaps your destiny lies in finding those that are lost."

Tarisio traveled to Cremona in the early 1800s to inquire about Stradivari and his violins. He was directed to Stradivari's granddaughter Francesca, a nun in a nearby church. She was thrilled to find that someone wanted to know about her grandfather's violins. She urged Luigi to look in churches, farmhouses, pawnshops, and among the effects of late musicians.

Then she told him of her grandfather's most perfect piece of workmanship, "the Messiah," which she had seen in her father's home when she was younger. The varnish was beautiful, and even though it was almost 100 years old, it would appear as if it had just been made. She knew that it had been sold, along with many other Stradivari violins, to Count Cozio di Salabue. Hopefully, she said to Tarisio, he could search it out and put it in a worthy player's hands.

Tarisio decided to devote his life to finding lost Cremonese violins and especially to recovering "the Messiah Strad." He traveled throughout Italy with several decoy violins in good playing condition. After introducing himself at a church or farmhouse as a wandering musician and passing some time in idle discussion, he would choose the proper time to inquire about old violins. Because he chose his stops carefully and he kept his true mission secret, Luigi's success was incredible. Many times his host would show him a battered Cremonese violin and Tarisio would counter with his "common fiddle" in perfect playing shape. After playing for a few minutes, a trade was negotiated and Tarisio would leave with a violin worth a fortune!

Luigi took these violins to Paris where dealers were astonished at his finds. He was the greatest violin connoisseur the world had ever seen, or will ever see, for no one will ever have his opportunity again.

It was the Parisian dealer Jean Baptiste Vuillaume who had the sense to realize that in Tarisio he had the source for some of the greatest instruments in the world. This was a man who, because of his personality, Italian blood, and knowledge of violins, could "pry away" violins from their owners while still giving them satisfaction. Vuillaume gave Luigi higher and higher prices for his finds to insure his confidence and to continue his search.

In his own land Tarisio remained nothing more than a quiet, unobtrusive repairman and collector of dilapidated violins. He lived in Milan in the attic of a second-class restaurant. His ploy of trading a new violin for an old one worked most of the time; but with professional musicians and collectors he was forced to trade more valuable instruments and pay in cash.

After trying for many years to work a deal with Count Cozio, Tarisio finally succeeded in 1827. Armed with the knowledge that the Count was especially fond of Amati violins, Luigi was able to tempt him with one of the finest Amatis ever made. Thus he obtained "the Messiah" Strad and a number of other Stradivari instruments in exchange for the Amati and cash. "The Messiah" was everything that Francesca said it was, and Tarisio mentioned it often, but never brought it with him when he visited Vuillaume.

*I*n 1854, when Tarisio had not been seen for several days, his neighbors became suspicious. When the knock at his door went unanswered, they broke in and found him dead, surrounded by violins piled high and low in chaotic fashion. The instant Vuillaume heard of his friend's death, he hurried to Milan to make the greatest purchase of his life. He acquired over 24 Strads, 120 violins made by lesser-known Italians, and "the Messiah," which was hidden away in a chest of drawers.

Once *Le Messie* was in Vuillaume's hands and he realized its importance, it was carefully guarded. Unlike any other Strad, it was in mint condition and completely covered with its original varnish. Vuillaume valued it at 480 pounds in 1875. After Vuillaume's death it passed though the hands of his son-in-law to the London firm of William Hill and Son, who valued it at 2000 pounds in 1890. The Hills left a lasting memorial to the glory of Stradivari by bequeathing the most perfect example of his art, "the Messiah" Strad, to the British nation. Today it is part of the rare instrument collection housed in the Ashmolean Museum in Oxford.

As major orchestras and soloists of the world present their Christmas concerts this year, many will include the soul of Stradivari. String players and music lovers will pause to remember the birth of the Messiah, the Son of God, born in Bethlehem nearly 2000 years ago. Many will also remember "the Messiah" Strad born in 1716 in Cremona, Italy, and other fine instruments made by Antonio Stradivari.

Christmas Music

New Carols for the Christmas Season

Let Us Sing Noel

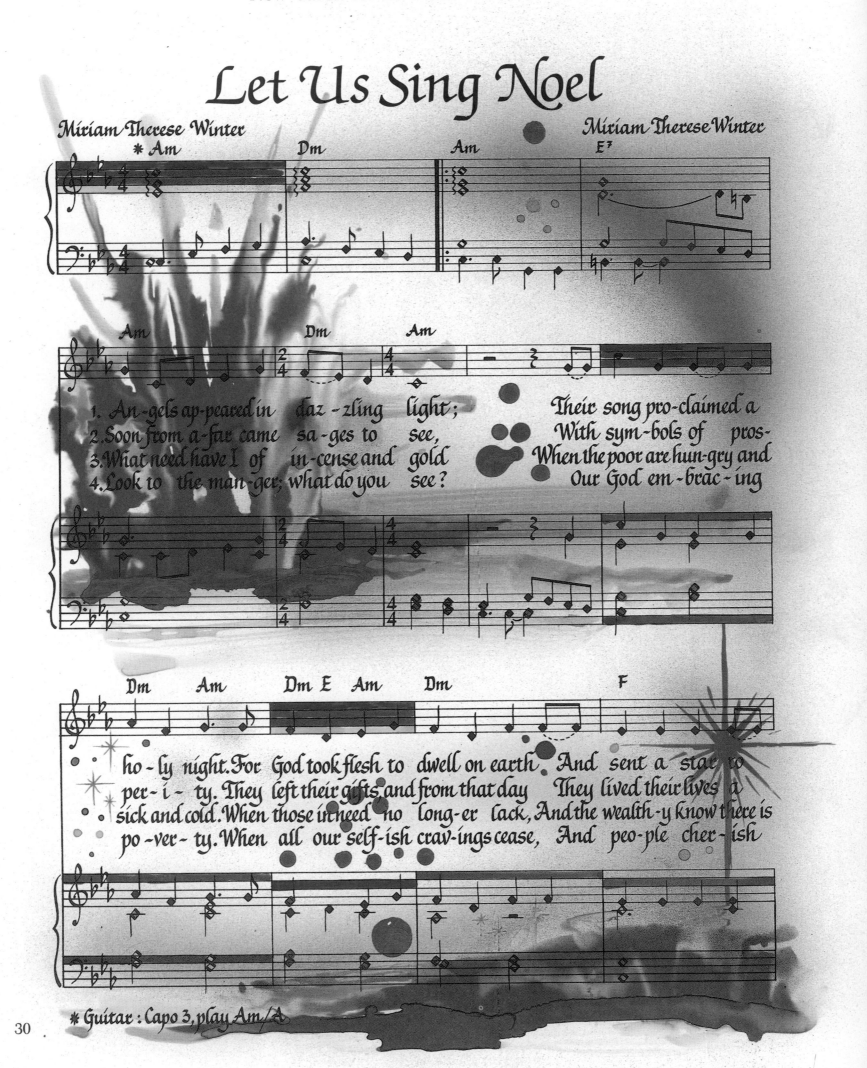

Miriam Therese Winter

Miriam Therese Winter

1. An-gels ap-peared in daz-zling light;   Their song pro-claimed a
2. Soon from a-far came sa-ges to see,   With sym-bols of pros-
3. What need have I of in-cense and gold   When the poor are hun-gry and
4. Look to the man-ger; what do you see?   Our God em-brac-ing

ho-ly night. For God took flesh to dwell on earth, And sent a star to
per-i-ty. They left their gifts, and from that day They lived their lives a-
sick and cold. When those in need no long-er lack, And the wealth-y know there is
po-ver-ty. When all our self-ish crav-ings cease, And peo-ple cher-ish

30   * Guitar : Capo 3, play Am/A

her-ald the birth, And shep-herds sang No ~ el.
dif-fer-ent way, And an-gels sang No ~ el.
no go-ing back, The poor will sing No ~ el.
jus-tice and peace, Then all will sing No ~ el.

Sing a song of ju-bi-la-tion, Word made flesh for our sal-va-tion,

Love in a man-ger, come and see: Hope in-hab-its his-to-ry. Oh,

let us sing No-el,_____ Let us sing No-el. ~ el.

Where Shepherds Lately Knelt

Jaroslav Vajda

Carl Schalk

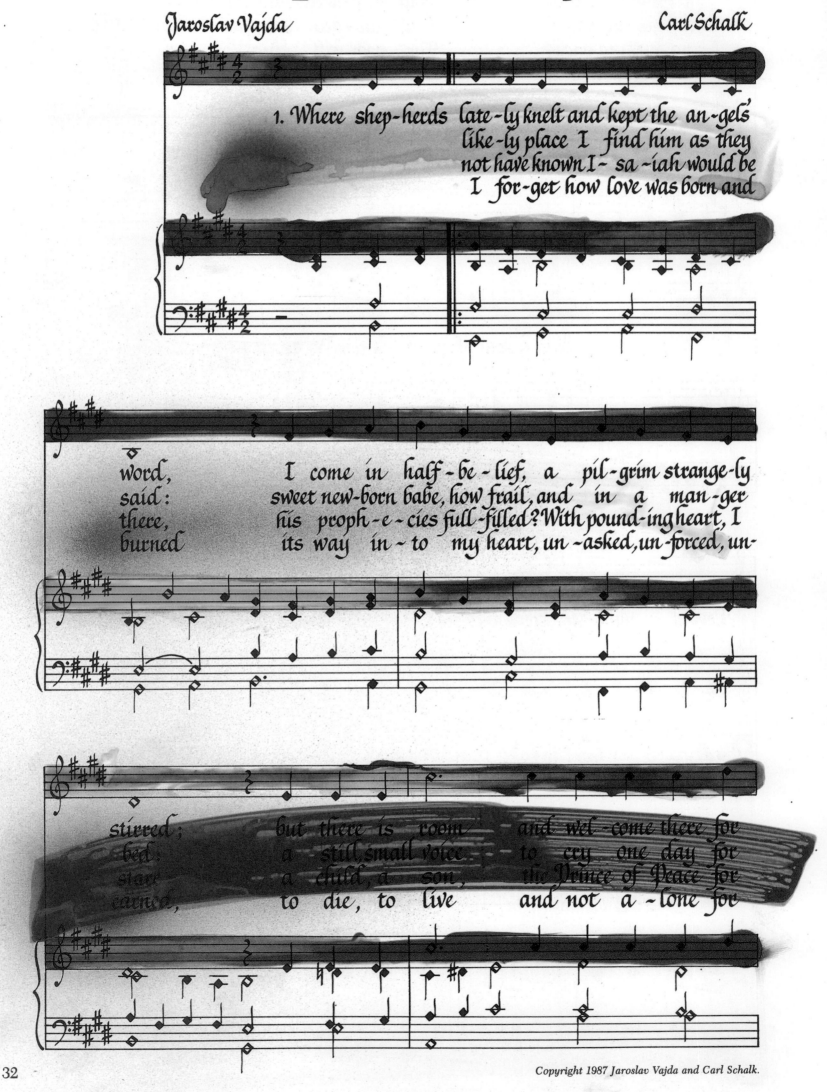

1. Where shep-herds late-ly knelt and kept the an-gels'
like-ly place I find him as they
not have known I~ sa~iah would be
I for-get how love was born and

word, I come in half~be~lief, a pil-grim strange-ly
said: sweet new-born babe, how frail, and in a man-ger
there, his proph-e~cies full~filled? With pound-ing heart, I
burned its way in~to my heart, un~asked, un~forced, un-

stirred; but there is room and wel~come there for
bed: a still, small voice to cry one day for
stare a child, a son, the Prince of Peace for
earned, to die, to live and not a~lone for

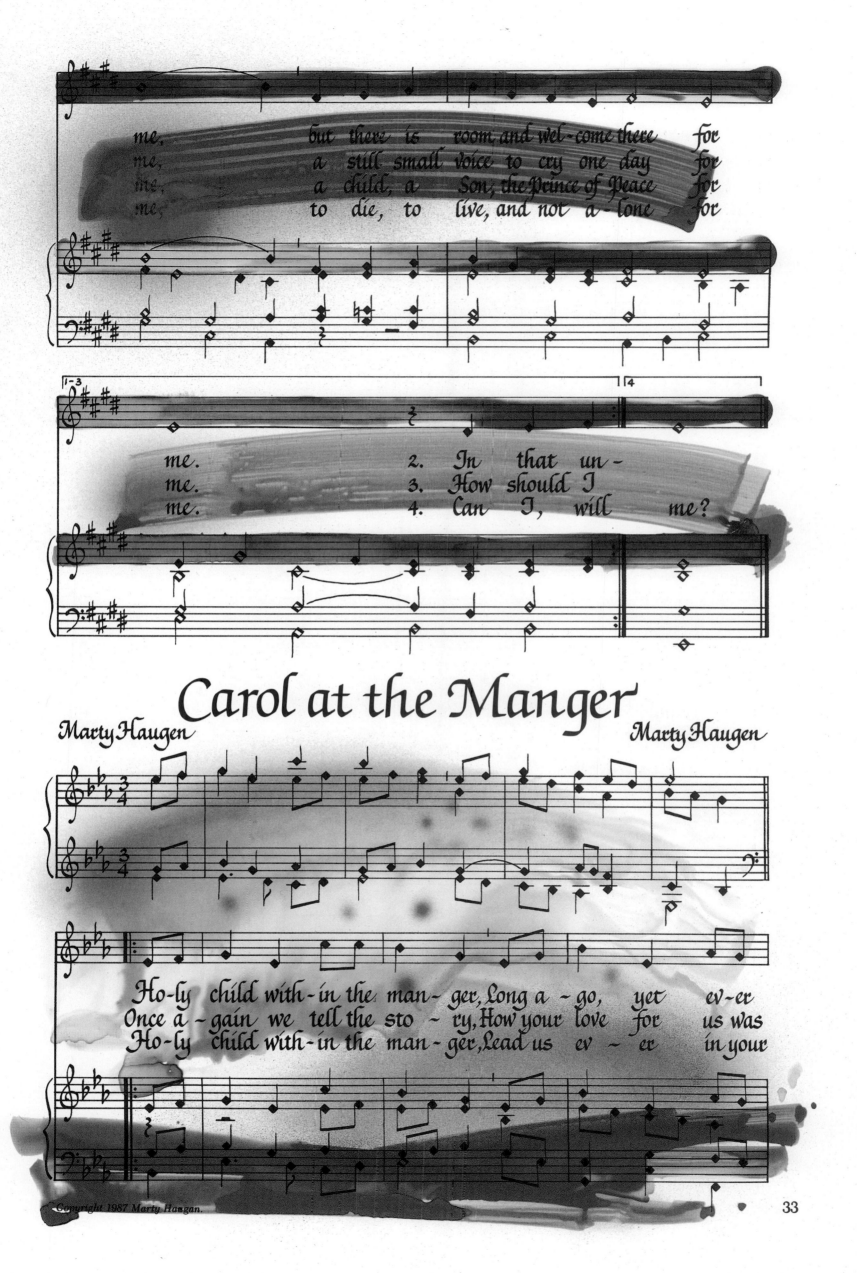

Carol at the Manger

Marty Haugen

Marty Haugen

Ho-ly child with-in the man-ger, Long a-go, yet ev-er
Once a-gain we tell the sto-ry, How your love for us was
Ho-ly child with-in the man-ger, Lead us ev-er in your

33

The Christ Child King

Come, Hear the Angel Chorus

Ron Klug

John Ferguson

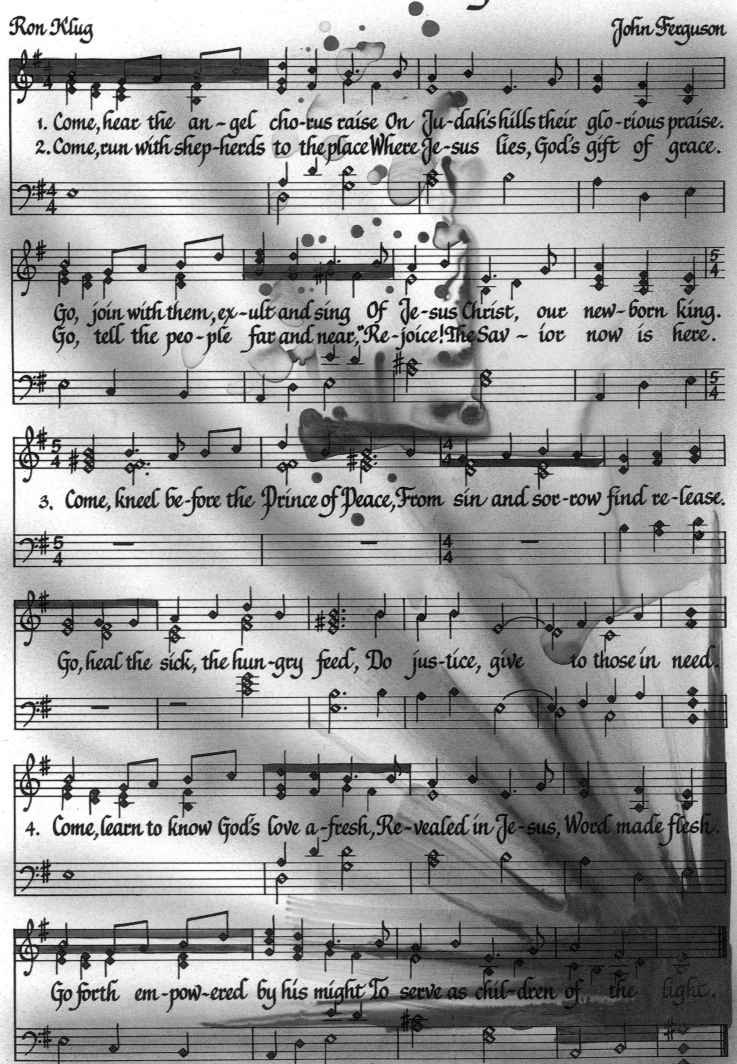

1. Come, hear the an-gel cho-rus raise On Ju-dah's hills their glo-rious praise.
2. Come, run with shep-herds to the place Where Je-sus lies, God's gift of grace.

Go, join with them, ex-ult and sing Of Je-sus Christ, our new-born king.
Go, tell the peo-ple far and near, "Re-joice! The Sav-ior now is here."

3. Come, kneel be-fore the Prince of Peace, From sin and sor-row find re-lease.

Go, heal the sick, the hun-gry feed, Do jus-tice, give to those in need.

4. Come, learn to know God's love a-fresh, Re-vealed in Je-sus, Word made flesh.

Go forth em-pow-ered by his might To serve as chil-dren of the light.

For the Sake of Him

Clayton J. Schmit   Clayton J. Schmit

1. With-in the child's hol-low face, Who goes to sleep each
2. With-in the with-ered hands of age, Whose fin-gers grasp in
3. With-in the wom-an's tear-filled eyes, Whose ill-ness is her
4. With-in the child's hap-py face, Whose smile is filled with

night un-fed, We see the Ba-by Je-sus' face, Who
lone-li-ness, We see the Ba-by Je-sus' hands, Who
great-est fear, We see the Ba-by Je-sus' eyes, Who
Christ-mas joy, We see the Ba-by Je-sus' face, The

hun-gered in a man-ger bed. And for the sake of
clutched up-on his moth-er's breast. And for the sake of
bathed him-self in ho-ly tears. And for the sake of
in-fant king, the ho-ly boy. And for the sake of

him who taught Our stone-filled hearts to care,
him who taught Our stone-filled hearts to care,
him who taught Our stone-filled hearts to care,
him who taught Our stone-filled hearts to care,

We are moved, we are moved our bread to share.
We are moved, we are moved our hearts to share.
We are moved, we are moved our hope to share.
We are moved, we are moved our joy to share.

37

Advent Supplication

ERLING J. GRUMSTRUP

Have patience, Advent, in your steadfast goal.
  Hasten not that I may, in conscience, find
The truth your message brings to humankind,
  And so prepare for Christmas in my soul.

Take heed, my soul, the season's heaven-sent;
  Pressing on through vain distractions of the day;
Beseeching justice, peace, and love along its way,
  Thus begins the ever-glorious Christ event.

Welcome, Christmas, and be rightly celebrated
  With angel chorus sung in joy and praise;
Might I hear their anthems and to heaven raise
  My song of gratitude for salvation now created.

Abide, O gentle spirit, holy Christmas child;
  Arouse my idle conscience out of apathy
That by your redeeming grace I might eternally
  In penitence with God be reconciled.

Biggest Little Thing in the World

ALLAN HAUCK

"The biggest little thing in the world" was the phrase Emily Bissell used to describe the Christmas seal. And she was right! The Christmas seal has literally changed the course of medical history; all because of the compassion of ordinary men and women committed to the struggle against one of humanity's oldest and deadliest enemies, tuberculosis.

Those who grew up a few decades ago in one of the innumerable small towns of America remember two harbingers of Christmas, both of which appeared unfailingly each year about the same time that the local newspaper began a countdown of shopping days left until Christmas. These two harbingers, however, did not represent the commercialism that so often obscures the real meaning of the season; instead, they personified the spirit of sharing our blessings with others. One was the ubiquitous Santa Claus who tirelessly rang his bell to solicit contributions for The Salvation Army; the other was the lady who placed her cardtable in the post office lobby or near the department store entrance to sell Christmas seals—often one at a time to youngsters, as well as in larger quantities to older people who still remembered the dread killer disease that the seals targeted. The Christmas seal throughout the years has raised millions of dollars and has become the primary source of funds for the American Lung Association, which often identifies itself simply as "The Christmas Seal People."

The story begins, however, in the later decades of the last century and in the first decade of this century. Tuberculosis was then a dread word, often whispered because a diagnosis of tuberculosis was usually received as a death sentence. It was variously called consumption, the White Plague, or simply TB and meant certain death for almost all its victims, whether they were senior citizens or youngsters.

Because of the success of the Christmas seal and of the medical research and care it funded, tuberculosis is no longer the incurable threat to life that it was at the beginning of this century. Indeed, it was as recent

as 1882 that Robert Koch discovered the tubercle bacillus. Medical science finally knew what caused the dread disease, but there was no cure!

So it was that when Dr. Edward Livingston Trudeau was diagnosed as having tuberculosis, he accepted this diagnosis as an irreversable death sentence and decided to spend his few remaining months or years in the Adirondack Mountains he had enjoyed so much as a youth. He retired to a simple cottage near Lake Saranac, and there a miracle happened. Instead of growing weaker, he began to feel better. He noticed that the more he rested, the better he felt. Based on his own experience, he pursued the idea that rest in an environment of fresh, pure air might be the cure for this dread disease. His cottage, or "shack" as it was called, was converted into a two-patient hospital. This became the nucleus for a larger establishment later called a sanitarium.

By 1904 enough American physicians were convinced of the importance of this cure that they formed the National Association for the Study and Prevention of Tuberculosis, a name that was shortened to the National Tuberculosis Association. It became the first voluntary health organization established to fight a specific disease. Tuberculosis is still a danger and thousands of Americans still suffer from it. Yet, the organization was so successful in banishing this ancient ravager of humanity, that in 1968 it expanded its focus and changed its name to the National Tuberculosis and Respiratory Disease Association, and again in 1973 to the American Lung Association. In less than 70 years it had evolved from a one-disease centered voluntary health agency into an organization willing to take on the multiple and complex adversaries to good lung health. Respiratory diseases still form the single largest cause of people visiting their physicians.

Appropriately enough, Dr. Tru-

Photos: A U.S. postage stamp honors Emily Bissell who introduced the Christmas seal to America. The very first Christmas seal featured Denmark's Queen Louise. "Father of the Christmas Seal," Einar Holboell, was portrayed on the 1927 Danish Christmas seal.

deau was elected the association's first president. As one who not only had discovered a cure but also had experienced it himself, he was a persuasive and dedicated leader during the early years of the association. This band of physicians felt that now they not only knew the germ that caused tuberculosis but they also had discovered a cure that could vanquish this age-old plague.

Even in the rarified realms of medical science, however, patterns of thought change slowly. Many physicians and most patients continued to think of tuberculosis as incurable; certainly a cure of rest, good food, and fresh air seemed too simple. The early members of the association felt that they were waging a war against a mystery murderer who struck people of all ages. For this reason they chose as their emblem a red double-barred cross patterned after the Lorraine Cross, which the Crusaders had used almost 800 years earlier. They, too, would be warriors in a health crusade!

Now our story shifts from America and the world of medicine to a postal worker in Denmark. As a child, Einar Holboell had dreamed of becoming a captain in the Danish navy, as his father had been, but rheumatic fever made this impossible. So he had settled for a job in the Danish civil service and found himself working in a post office. He was saddened by the fact that some children whom he knew and loved had contracted tuberculosis. But he also had read of the success of the new rest cure that was being tried in the United States. He wished that a hospital could be built in Denmark for children with tuberculosis.

One day at work an idea came to him! As a postal employee, he knew that people tended to show a more loving and caring spirit at Christmastime. Cards and gifts kept the post office busier than at any other time of the year. Perhaps funds to fight tuberculosis could be raised through Christmas stamps—sold not to pay postal charges but to support the fight against tuberculosis. In this manner everyone—young, old, rich, poor—could contribute to the defeat of this ancient enemy.

Holboell's idea was enthusiastically received and in 1904 the world's first Christmas stamps were sold in Denmark. The first stamp featured Denmark's Queen Louise encircled by a wreath of roses. These first Christmas stamps originally sold for 2 öre and netted over 74,000 kroner. Einar Holboell's compassion for the youthful victims of tuberculosis in Denmark had set in motion what would prove to be one of the world's most successful fundraising programs.

In just a few years it could be said that all over the world the little stamps had become bullets in the war on the White Plague, which humanity was at last winning. (In the early years the term "stamps" was used, but gradually they came to be called "seals" to avoid any confusion with postage.)

By the time of his death in 1927 Holboell had already become known as the "Father of the Christmas Seal." His portrait was featured on the 1927 seal in honor of his work in battling tuberculosis. Later, a statue was erected to his memory in Charlottenlund, where he had served as postmaster. The statue was financed, appropriately enough, with funds raised by children who sold a special seal all over Denmark.

When the first Christmas seal proved such an immediate success, humanitarians in Sweden and Iceland

Christmas Seals Through the Years

The first American Christmas seal was designed by Emily Bissell herself in 1907. The next year the American Red Cross agreed to sponsor the campaign.

The 1920 seal included the double-barred Cross of Lorraine as a trademark. The rescue of children from tuberculosis is illustrated on the 1922 seal.

Twenty-five years of battle against tuberculosis are commemorated on this 1931 Christmas seal.

The two color variations in this pair of 1936 seals were a departure from the one-design tradition.

This colorful sampling of Christmas seals from the 1940s and 1951 portray a variety of Christmas greeters— from carolers to Santa Claus.

The corresponding halves of this double seal from 1958 bring Christmas greetings and introduce a design concept used on later seals.

The whimsical house and snowman on the 1963 seals were reversed to create a block of four different Christmas seals.

became excited about the seal's potential and acted quickly to release their first Christmas seals that same year. Year after year tuberculosis associations in more and more countries climbed on the bandwagon and produced their own seals. In 1907 the first Christmas seal was released in America. The story of the American seal is the story of one woman's dedication and determination, which literally changed the course of the battle against tuberculosis in the United States.

A letter bearing one of the first Danish Christmas seals had come into the hands of Jacob Riis, a Danish-American writer whom Theodore Roosevelt once called "America's most useful citizen." He, in turn, had written an article for an American magazine in which he told the story of the Christmas seal's success and encouraged Americans to introduce this successful fund-raiser in their struggle against the White Plague. Riis had personal knowledge of the toll tuberculosis took; it had killed six of his brothers! Then, too, in his first years in America he had lived in tenements and knew firsthand the danger of contagious diseases in overcrowded tenements and sweatshops. His autobiography, *How the Other Half Lives*, led New York state to pass legislation to control tenement abuses. His little magazine article about the Danish Christmas seals was, however, destined to have an even greater impact on American health.

On the American scene, success in rallying general support for the new cure would rest not so much on medical organizations as upon the shoulders of one committed and determined woman, Emily Bissell. In 1907 the Brandywine Shack, a cottage-hospital on the banks of the Brandywine River in Delaware that cared for eight charity patients and was staffed by a nurse and a cook, was on the verge of closing because of insufficient funds. One of the physicians associated with the small hospital solicited the aid of his cousin, Emily Bissell, who was active in the Delaware Red Cross and was an experienced fund raiser. She had just read Jacob Riis' magazine article on the success of the Danish Christmas seals with his appeal that this scheme be used in America. Here was a chance for her to test the fund-raising capabilities of the Christmas seal!

Emily also had another use in mind for the Christmas seal. Besides raising financial support for the care of tubercular patients, it would educate the general public, as well as conservative physicians, to the idea that tuberculosis was no longer incurable. Only a handful of people believed it could really be cured; most still thought it was hereditary and invincible. The Christmas seal could be the messenger of the glad tidings that medicine had really found a cure! In an effort to save the small open-air tuberculosis shack near the Brandywine (built on land leased from Alfred J. duPont for a dollar a year), Emily Bissell was about to launch a scheme that would eventually raise millions of dollars each year and become the primary support of the American Lung Association.

Emily moved quickly. She received approval from the Delaware Red Cross to use their logo, and the post office gave her permission to put a stand in the post office lobby. She designed the first seal herself. It was a simple holly garland with the words "Merry Christmas" (the year was not shown). She found a printer, Charles Story, who agreed to print 50,000 seals in red (two-color printing would have been too expensive) and "await results for payment." He also printed 2000 small envelopes to hold 25 seals each. They read:

Put this stamp with message bright
On every Christmas letter;
Help the tuberculosis fight,
And make the New Year better.
These stamps do not carry any kind of mail
but any kind of mail will carry them.

Now everything was ready. At noon on Saturday, December 7, 1907, Miss Lillie Ray, in a nurse's uniform, took her place at the temporary table erected in the lobby of the Wilmington post office and made the first sale of America's first Christmas seals to Emily Bissell, their creator.

The sales that first day came to less than $25.00 and the sales on following days were also disappointing. Local shopkeepers were not encouraging because they felt people could buy more attractive seals for much less. Emily, however, didn't give up. She decided that what was needed for success was more publicity and a larger market. Therefore, on December 11, Emily boarded the train for Philadelphia where she planned to seek the support of *The North American*, a newspaper that was read widely in Delaware.

Miss Bissell recalls that the Sunday editor, whose support she sought, was "polite" but "visibly shocked at the thought of coupling 'Merry Christmas' with the worst of diseases." Crestfallen, she was leaving the newspaper building when she impulsively decided to visit Leigh Mitchell Hodges, whose daily column, "The Optimist," she read regularly. Hodges responded enthusiastically to the cause that had brought Emily to the newspaper and took a sheet of the seals to his editor-in-chief, E. A. Van Valkenburg, who was so taken by Hodges' enthusiasm and his suggestion of the slogan "Stamp Out Tuberculosis" that he told the columnist to drop everything else he was doing and to take as much space as he needed to support this cause.

When the 1907 sales were concluded, the campaign had realized more than $3000, 10 times more than was needed to keep the Brandywine Shack operating. In the face of such spontaneous success the national headquarters of the American Red Cross agreed to sponsor the Christmas seal campaign the following year. This partnership continued until 1920 when the National Tuberculosis Association was strong enough to take over. From 1919 the double-barred Cross of Lorraine has appeared on Christmas seals as the trademark of the association.

The Christmas seal, which so gracefully adds a note of care and love to our Christmas cards and letters, is still doing its job. It is the primary source of income for the American Lung Association, which having practically achieved its original goal—the cure and prevention of tuberculosis—has now turned its attention to other diseases of the lung, that truly vital and extraordinary organ without which human life cannot exist. Ironically enough, in spite of the near conquest of tuberculosis in America, respiratory diseases are still the most frequent reason for people seeing their physicians. Emphysema, chronic bronchitis, pneumonia, influenza, occupational lung diseases, and pediatric asthma are now as common, or even more common, than tuberculosis used to be.

A quartet of scarlet tanagers sing their Christmas greetings on these seals from 1966.

A trainload of holiday cheer arrived with the 1967 Christmas seal.

Borrowing from a popular song, the 1973 seals illustrated gifts for the 12 days of Christmas.

Detail from the 1976 full-page scenic Christmas seal.

Paintings by American schoolchildren were reproduced as Christmas seals in the years 1975, 1977, 1978, 1979, and 1980.

In 1982 package labels were added to the Christmas seal sheet along with the traditional theme seals.

The 1986 Christmas seal introduced Kristy Koala, the new mascot for the American Lung Association.

With 350,000 Americans dying each year from smoking-related diseases and with the miracle of breath going wrong for the 18½ million Americans who suffer from some form of chronic lung disease, there is still a need for an association devoted to lung research, care, and education.

The 1986 Christmas seals introduced a cartoon character named Kristy Koala, the first mascot ever chosen by the American Lung Association. Two years earlier the wife of the managing director of the American Lung Association had given him a stuffed bear as a Valentine's Day gift. As a personalizing touch, she had dressed the bear in a needlepoint bib bearing the words, "Hug Me, I Don't Smoke." From this, James A. Swomley, the American Lung Association managing director, got the idea for a mascot and he called an old friend at Mattel Inc. for help.

A year later they selected the koala, a marsupial rather than a bear, because this animal is so susceptible to respiratory infections and because the last three letters in koala are the same as the initials for the American Lung Association. Kristy Koala, presented in four attractive poses on the 1986 Christmas seals, may well become one of the standard yuletide personalities. Along with its appearance on approximately 2½ billion Christmas seals, the mascot appeared in a whole line of Mattel products, of which the most huggable was a 10½-inch plush Kristy wearing a bib emblazoned with the message: "Hug Me. I Don't Smoke!" Mattel contributed a portion of all Kristy product sales to the American Lung Association's educational program for the prevention of smoking among young people.

Finally, it should be noted that as the years have passed the Christmas seals have brought an unexpected, derivative kind of joy to many people for whom they have become collectibles. Most of them are not too expensive. Copies of the first 1904 Danish Christmas seal and the 1907 United States Christmas seal are obtainable for around $10.00. Like stamps, seals come in many collectible varieties—color variations, color omissions, missing perforations, color proofs, full sheets, complete booklets, and even printer's waste (mistakes). Many collectors of Christmas seals share their collections with others by displaying them in banks, post offices, and churches during the Christmas season. They also have formed a national association devoted to the collecting and studying of these seals. A collection of Christmas seals is not only a thing of beauty but is also a witness to the struggle for health and happiness that these seals originally represented.

Emily Bissell used to say, the seals have "given everyone a chance to be of real help in the defense and spread of health and happiness." The ragged Philadelphia newsboy, too small to see over the counter, who in 1907 reached up to thrust his penny over the counter with the words, "Gimme one, my sister's got it," has long symbolized the success of the Christmas seal movement. It depends upon each one of us and upon our compassion and love for others.

Next time you use a Christmas seal, remember that you are part of a crusade against all the diseases that attack the human lung. Your seal bears testimony that the human heart is moved by the Christmas gospel to give the gift of life.

Lithuania

Christmas on the Baltic

Christmas Celebrations in Lithuania, Latvia, and Estonia

LA VERN J. RIPPLEY

The Baltic states comprise a group of three former nations that share a common prehistoric culture, that of the Balts. Today they form the Soviet republics of Lithuania, Latvia, and Estonia. Geographically they are situated east of the Baltic Sea, which also washes the shores of Sweden, Denmark, Germany, Poland, and Finland. Although incorporated against their wishes into the Soviet Union, the three Baltic states since time immemorial have harbored their own traditions, folk customs, and special Christian beliefs. We shall consider the Baltic Christmas and New Year's folk traditions together, as all three states are successors to the original Balts.

The three republics enjoy a moderate climate more characteristic of central Europe than of the hot summers and bitter winters of inland Soviet Union. Also, European deciduous and coniferous trees, arable croplands, and domestic animals are more commonplace here than in the Soviet heartland. The songs of the nightingale and the nesting of storks atop farmers' houses symbolize the affinity of the villagers to life-bringing natural forces. The seasonal rotation, language, beliefs, customs, and traditions have remained as unchanged here as the birds and the animals in the forests. Low houses with thatched roofs exemplify the use of naturally grown materials for everyday living. Homes look like mushrooms that have sprung up naturally out of the earth.

In the fields and pastures, shepherd children play their flutes, quaint wooden pipes. With the family gathered around the hearth during the long winter nights or seated around a mother's spinning wheel, folksongs are sung and embellished from one generation to the next. Lullabies and wedding songs, lamentations at wakes, hymns and carols sung during church services and at Christmas observances, all indicate that singing for the Balts is as necessary as breathing. According to some statistics, Latvians and Lithuanians alone have at least a half million collected folksongs, reflecting the intimate kinship felt between the earth and its many creatures. It is against this pastoral background that we view the customs associated with the close and rebirth of the year.

The Baltic states were determined geographically by their river valleys—the Memel, the Daugave, and others—by their lakes, and by the rocky, sandy soil left in a morraine by the last ice age. To the south, the swampy Pripet River Basin demarcated them from Byelorussia. But, lacking any natural barriers to the east and lying open to the sea on the west, the Baltic states have always been vulnerable to foreign invasions. Each new wave of invaders influenced the year-end festivities of the Balts, but none succeeded in replacing the ethnic customs.

Ruled at the dawn of history by powerful chieftains and landlords, the Balts assumed a central role between the Scandinavians to the west, the Kievans to the east, and the Byzantines to the south. Coming at them from the southwest were the Germans with their roots in the Latin traditions of Rome. Despite early efforts from the east, Christian traditions for the celebration of Christmas did not reach the Baltic countries until the thirteenth century, and then only through missionaries who accompanied the Teutonic Knights. In southernmost Lithuania, an organized Christian church was in place by 1387; but for centuries thereafter pagan practices continued. Gradually, the Catholic church acquiesced by adopting the pagan traditions of the peasantry. During the Reformation the Lithuanian peasant remained noncommittal, caring neither for the Protestant nor for the Catholic administrator, until about 1650 when the Lithuanians cast their lot with the Poles in favor of Rome. Today about 75 percent of Lithuanians are Catholic, 10 percent are Lutheran, and the remainder are a mixture including Russian Orthodox people brought in by Soviet rulers to diffuse the ethnicity of the Lithuanians.

Latvians, by comparison, are over 60 percent Lutheran and 25 percent Roman Catholic, with a smattering of other religions making up the balance. Since World War II, Soviet authorities have seen to it that in the Latvian population of about 3.5 million, about 30 percent of the people have been resettled from elsewhere in the Soviet Union.

Considerably less populated than Latvia is Estonia, having a mere 1.5 million people in 1975. Of these, likewise, some 25 percent are immigrants from the Soviet heartland. Christianity was slow in gaining the upper hand in Estonia, though efforts were made by monks from Bremen, Germany, as early as 1180. The first real success at conversion came with Bishop Albert I (d. 1229) who imposed Christianity and renamed the area

Latvia

Metcalf

Marienland ("Land of the Blessed Virgin"). Partly as a revolt against episcopal authority and partly due to internal political maneuvering, Estonia turned to Lutheranism after the onset of Swedish rule around 1600. In Estonia during the 1930s about 78 percent of the ethnic population was Lutheran, while about 19 percent was Orthodox—that is, before the Soviet introduction of outsiders to dilute the ethnic people. Regardless of which brand of Christianity held sway, the fact remains that heathen rituals and customs persisted and do to this day.

Christmas has been celebrated in the Baltic countries for centuries, but always as an eclectic affair that bore much resemblance to pre-Christian festivals. This fact is the key to understanding the Baltic year-end holidays. Antiquity holds sway in their beliefs, hymns, carols, and folksongs. The comparatively recent Christian era amounts to little more than a veneer over the ancient culture.

Lithuania

The Lithuanian Christmas, *Kucios*, encompasses the regular Advent season common to all of Christian Europe. December 24, however, is the most sacred day. Certain superstitions have long governed what could and could not be done on this day before Christmas. In general, work connected with preparation for the feast itself is the only activity allowed. Especially forbidden is the use of a handmill to grind flour because this is thought to bring destructive thunderstorms the following summer, which no farmer can risk. It is also an ill omen to spin, patch garments, or to chop wood on Christmas Eve. These actions portend evil not only for people but also for domestic animals. In the tradition of their Polish neighbors, Lithuanians fast all day on December 24 until the first evening star appears in the heavens. Then it is time for the family to sit down to a traditional meal. If relatives cannot be present or, perhaps, have passed away, then an empty place is left for them at the table.

Immediately under the tablecloth on which this meal is served lays a bed of straw or hay, placed there to symbolize the birth of Christ in a stable. On Christmas Day itself, Lithuanians feed this hay to the animals to insure their productivity for the following year.

At the Christmas Eve dinner, however, the crucial serving is the *plotka*, an unleavened wheat wafer usually made and distributed for this special meal by the churches. After saying grace the family head breaks the wafer and hands a piece to all persons present as a symbol of togetherness. No meat or dairy products may be served on Christmas Eve, although fish (often herring or pike) is common, in keeping with the tradition of fasting and abstinence during the Advent season. The principal dish on Christmas Eve is *kucia*, a mixture of cooked whole grains of wheat, barley, oats, and peas. This is brewed in a liquid consisting of water, honey, milk, and ground poppy seeds. Other dishes might include red beet soup, hard baked dumplings, and mushrooms.

Food not consumed by the family that evening is left on the table overnight to be enjoyed by deceased members of the family or by the family of Jesus, his angels, or disciples. That same evening the farm animals are given their own special *kucia*, an ample measuring of hay, oats, and other grains. At midnight in Lithuania, animals are thought to kneel and pray, or even speak. But if anyone intentionally listens to what they say, it is feared he or she will surely die within the year. At midnight, it is assumed that water in wells turns to wine, bees in their hives predict the future, and sheep by their behavior signal bad or good omens for the coming year. Hens, likewise, lay extra eggs. Sometimes family members take a bit of straw left from the table decoration and bundle up fruit trees to protect them from the cold during the winter and to assure a good harvest the next fall.

These activities indicate a desire to predict the future. On Christmas Eve some families call forth ancient rites to determine such things as how long each one will live, what kind of death awaits them, what good fortune might be in the offing, who will be the future husbands of young girls, and what the weather will be like during the coming seasons. Illustrating a curious mix of paganism and Christianity, witches are thought to roam through the region on Christmas Eve, and people take many precautions not to fall under their spell.

Christmas Day in the Lithuanian setting is a time for rest, for singing hundreds of carols, for eating good food, and for enjoying the company of family members. Nobody goes visiting on Christmas Day itself. But groups of schoolchildren often perform neighborhood plays, such as "Biblical Shepherds," "Old Man Christmas," "The Three Kings," or "The Old Year." These scenes are enacted as the children travel from house to house asking for a donation, usually of food. Equally entertaining are the children's Christmas disguises: "Leading a Bear," "Flying a Crane," plus many others that incorporate sham weddings and satires against village officials or, perhaps, school authorities.

On the day after Christmas, also known as Third Christmas, a "Day of Hail" is observed. On this day neighbors visit each other and celebrate in public. But it is considered bad luck if the first visitor to a household on Third Christmas is a woman.

New Year's Eve is in some respects a repeat of Christmas Eve, especially with reference to divinations concerning the coming year. Yet New Year's is never quite the boisterous event in Lithuania that it is in western European countries, partly because Lithuanians celebrate continously from the third day of Christmas right up to Epiphany on January 6. This period is called *tarpusventis*, literally "between the festivals," something comparable to the Twelve Nights in the English tradition. In many Lithuanian communities this entire period is used for games, masquerades, merrymaking, and general celebrations.

Many homes in modern times have adopted the Christmas tree, *kaledu eglute*, although this twentieth century development was once better known as the "wedding tree," a symbol of youth and fertility that was hung from the ceiling over the couple as they partook of the bridal banquet. Later the tree was made of straw; it survives today in the form of straw decorations on the

Estonia

Christmas tree and around the home. Santa Claus, too, has made his appearance in the Lithuanian setting, particularly among immigrants in the United States. He delivers gifts in the usual manner, but is not to be confused with *Kaleda*, the personification of Christmas and its festivities. *Kaleda* is conceived as an old man arriving from far away who knocks on a cottage door and speaks the introductory lines: "I am *Kaleda* and I bring happiness, a good harvest, and well-being."

Latvia

Latvia, like Lithuania, has been constantly under the pressure of either czars or Soviet rulers to conform to Russian ways. And Latvia, too, has struggled valiantly and successfully to preserve its own traditions and folkways. Much of this achievement must be ascribed to the maintenance of the Baltic language and, especially, the beloved folklore, folksongs, and folk traditions. Until the nineteenth century all of these were passed on by word of mouth only.

Much symbolism from ancient times persists in the lyrics of folksongs. At the basis of their message is a division of the solar year into eight seasons, called the Annual Order of Festivals. Each season has a proper name and 45 days. The festivals occur during the year at the commonly recognized positions of the sun, beginning with the winter solstice and followed by the spring equinox, the summer solstice, and the autumn equinox. The midpoints between each of these events also is designated as a festival. Because these festival periods add up to only 360 days, the winter solstice festival is increased by three days at the outset of winter and by two days at its conclusion. Since these days are needed, so to speak, for festivities anyway, this is the most pleasant way possible to square out the number of days needed for each year.

Following a policy begun by Pope Gregory I in 601, Christendom tried to spread its tenets by retaining the folk festivals and traditions and by superimposing Christian values and interpretations. The celebration of Christmas in Latvia, therefore, was combined with the ancient winter festival of *Ziemassvetki*, by far the most elaborate of the Annual Order of Festivals. Even in ancient times, this feast was designed to commemorate the time of *Dievs* ("God's birth"). This period of the winter solstice signified the arrival of the celestial beings, the *Dievaldeli*, four brothers who represented the number of days allotted for this celebration. Since earliest times, their image was that of prosperous bringers of gifts.

In many communities the Latvian Christmas begins according to the Order of Festivals on November 10, the midpoint between the fall equinox and the winter solstice. This is also the celebration of St. Martin's Day or *Martini*. Traditions appropriate to this feast can be celebrated anytime during the pre-Christmas season. Masked processions bring out merrymakers disguised in costumes and accompanied by much singing, dancing, and colorful joviality. The marchers vigorously pound homemade noisemakers as they advance from house to house, visiting friends and neighbors. Typical disguises are bears, gypsies, horses, storks, a personified sheaf of grain, and, in some instances, even the figure of death. According to tradition, the masqueraders represent holy spirits who bring good luck and fertility to people, fields, and flocks.

Fire is also an integral part of the Christmas celebration in Latvia. Thus, candles are used to symbolize the birth of Christ and, perhaps, of the sun. Fire symbolism is also prominent in the annual yule log ceremony. In many communities, the yule log is dragged from village to village by masqueraders, then burned at the last stop. Or it may be fetched first on Christmas Eve, as is more common in the English tradition. At any rate, burning the yule log in the Latvian tradition symbolizes more than warmth and good cheer. It also connotes the destruction of sorrows and misfortunes of the past year. Ancient Latvian custom also holds that the burning log helps the sun to recover its glow and to deliver happiness during the coming year, somewhat like priming a pump with water. In rural areas, a whole village may gather to pull the log from one farmstead to the next before the people gather for the ceremonial burning that night. During the fiery ritual, special folksongs or carols, called *kaladu*, are sung with refrains.

On Christmas Eve, Latvian families retire to their inner circle where a special feast awaits them. As they sit down to table, an empty place is left at the head to symbolize the presence of *Dievs* (God) in their midst. An abundance of traditional dishes deck the Latvian table—pork, especially pig's snout and pig's feet, plus a wide variety of breads, rolls, and fruit-filled Christmas pastries. Whole-grain dishes, as well as beans and peas, are also common.

In Catholic regions, midnight mass was once a powerful event following the Christmas Eve meal. In Lutheran districts, church services were usually part of the Christmas Day observances. Today, however, Soviet officials have done their best to minimize Christian worship during this special season.

Some communities engage in group fortune-telling, both at Christmas and on New Year's Eve. First a large bonfire is built and lead is heated to a molten state. Then the lead is poured in a thin stream into a barrel of cold water so that the droplets solidify instantly. Quite in keeping with the tradition of fire and light, Latvians hold up the lead formations in the firelight, thus casting shadows on a wall. From these distorted, haphazard formations, adults extrapolate future events and the prospects for good crops and happiness in the forthcoming year.

Anchored in this light-fire ritual is the tradition of masquerading. Identities hidden, groups of children march from house to house, bringing good cheer or telling the fortunes of their hosts with messages from "the realm of the shades." Mostly they offer a theme of prosperity and good fortune.

Estonia

Estonia was settled by Finno-Ugric people from East Asia, unlike the Balts who were indigenous to the regions of Prussia, Lithuania, and Latvia. But a similar pattern of conversion to Christianity, a parallel folk culture, and comparable historical experiences have resulted in Estonian traditions for the holidays that closely resemble those of Latvia and Lithuania.

The Estonian Christmas season has nominal Scandinavian features. The words for both Christmas, *joulud*, and New Year's, *naaripaev*, were borrowed undoubtedly during the Viking period from the Scandinavian languages. The comparable words in Swedish, for example, are *jul* ("Christmas") and *nyar* ("New Year"). Due to subsequent German influence, beginning with the Teutonic Knights and continuing through some 400 years of Hanseatic traders, the Christmas tree, gingerbreads, and later Santa Claus or Father Christmas were introduced.

*A*ncient Estonian Christmas traditions reflect the sacrificial peasant rituals of offering up the firstfruits of grains and field crops gathered either at the onset or at the conclusion of the harvest season. Thus, the first sheaves cut in the field are thought to have special powers. Stored in the threshing barn, each is given its own name and is to be used during the year at the celebration of some feast. For Christmas, there are specially named sheaves. These are harvested on Oolja Day, or St. Olaf's Day (July 29). On Christmas Eve, one of these ceremonial sheaves is brought in from the barn and placed on the dinner table. In order to guarantee a good harvest the following season, this sheaf is treated like a deity. It is offered the best beer in the house and is served the finest food from the Christmas Eve spread.

After the family finishes celebrating the Christmas holidays, the sheaf is returned ceremoniously to the barn where it is hung to protect the domestic herd through the winter months. Not until the following Oolja Day is the sheaf taken from its privileged post and fed to the cattle, thereby assuring the fertility and productivity of the domestic animals on the farm.

Also from the Oolja Day sheaves of grain is made the traditional Christmas bread known as *kollikakk*. In some families, the Christmas sheaf is brought in on harvest day and hung on the ceiling over the table to dry. On Christmas Eve the head of the household plucks a few straws from the hanging sheaf, tosses them into the air, and from their landing positions predicts the future course of events.

From these ceremonies of the sheaves it can readily be ascertained how the pagan spirit of fertility, which supposedly dwells in the sheaf, is enhanced by the Christian tradition. The grain symbolizes the body of Christ, the Eucharist, which shelters and protects Estonian believers. The powerful interweaving of God, humankind, and nature is suggested also by the different names given the sheaves—among them the pig, the threshing-barn caretaker, and the bogey man (a pagan, godlike spirit).

From St. Martin's Day until Epiphany, but especially during the 12 central days of Christmas, villagers in Estonia travel in troupes from homestead to homestead masquerading as animals—such as St. Martin's ram, St. Catherine's goose, New Year's billy goat, all figures that are intended to bring success during the coming year.

In some Estonian villages the Christmas goose (*jouluhani*) ganders from home to home dressed in a sheepskin coat on select evenings before Christmas, something like the German St. Nicholas and Ruprecht figures. The goose's threatening beak remains wide open to snap at mischievous little ones. If a proper costume is not available, then two fingers spread wide at the end of a long coat sleeve achieve the same effect. This Christmas goose has the function of warning children to be on their best behavior for Christmas Eve.

In a similar vein during the post-Christmas holidays, marchers carry fertility dolls made of straw. Called *metsik*, these dolls are often used for Christmas decorations in the home. Although their origin is now lost in antiquity, the name means approximately "the wild one" or "the one from the forest" and is considered to be a male figure. In some areas the dolls are also paraded through the fields in the spring to bring fertility to the land, after which the "used" dolls are deposited on a tree in a nearby forest to return to nature. In a few Estonian localities the doll is called *toorus*, suggesting the Scandinavian deity Thor. Some villages also have separate *metsik* celebrations, which, however, follow closely after Christmas and always are concluded before *Shrovetide*.

Visits are carried out ceremoniously with the help of masks and disguises. Thus the Christmas buck (*joulupukk*) or the New Year's buck (*naarisokk*) and the Epiphany she-goat (*kolmekuninga-kits*) are figures represented among the guests. Often the lad playing a buck's part wears either horns from a genuine buck or a conical straw hat from which horns plaited of straw branch out. On New Year's Day, in particular, young men put on sheepskin coats and stride about on hobby horses decked out with a buck's head instead of a horse's. Led by a herdsman they tour from house to house making noise, banging on pans, ringing bells, and baaing in the animal manner. When doors open they shout a New Year's wish tinged with fertility symbols: "May the hens lay eggs, the sheep beget twin lambs, the horses male colts, and the girls get married." Then they throw peas on the floor and are rewarded with beer and something to eat. Knit mittens or socks might also be hung on their horns as presents. In the more carnival-like village atmosphere, this merrymaking sometimes amounts to little more than frightening children, teasing girls, and enjoyable frolicking in the winter outdoors.

*D*uring the current era of suppression by Soviet rulers Christmas traditions, like Christianity itself, have gone somewhat dormant. But this period of winter is not likely to last forever. Even as domination by Teutonic Knights, Swedish overlords, and Roman bishops has in each instance proved futile, so it is improbable that the oppression of the moment will succeed in snuffing out the ancient Baltic folklore. In fact, the message of hope that the Christmas story brings annually might best be applied to the fate of these proud peoples. History is bound to repeat itself. Freedom and the open celebration of Christmas, like the springtime sun, will someday return in all their glory.

Christmas Shopping in a Country Store

BY BOB ARTLEY

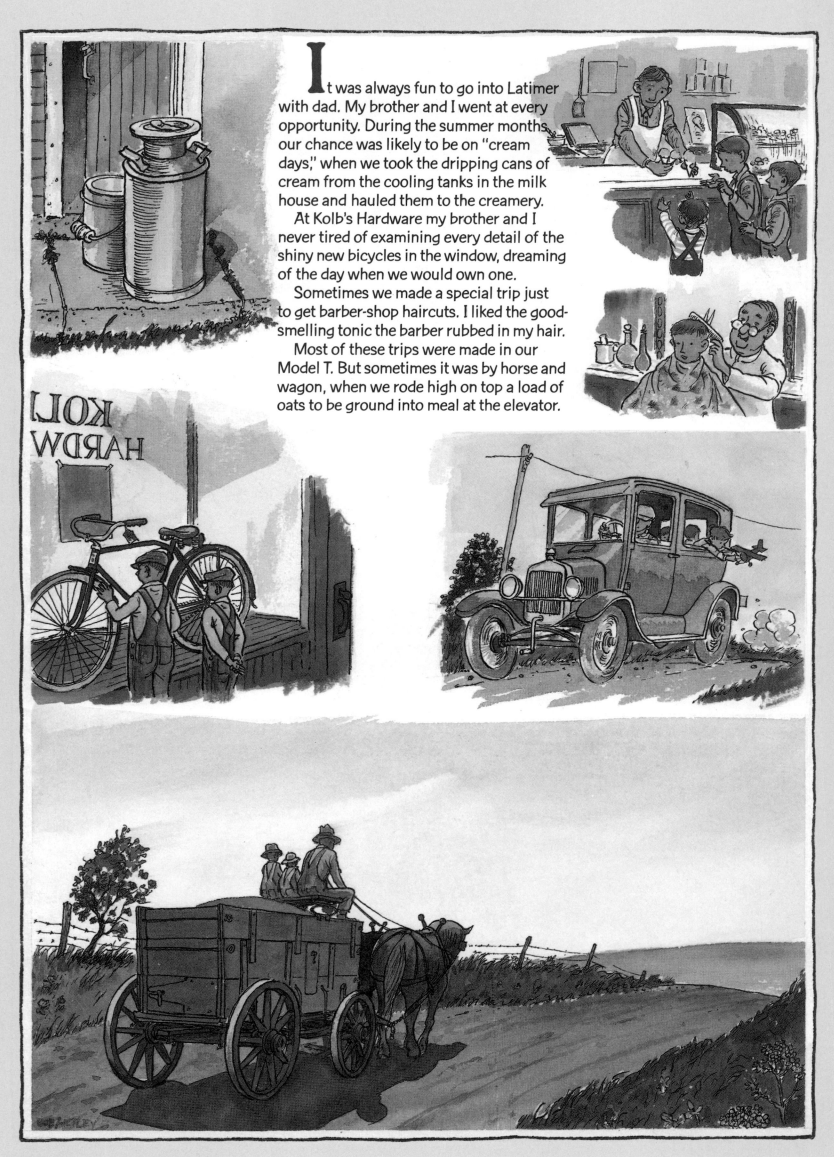

It was always fun to go into Latimer with dad. My brother and I went at every opportunity. During the summer months our chance was likely to be on "cream days," when we took the dripping cans of cream from the cooling tanks in the milk house and hauled them to the creamery.

At Kolb's Hardware my brother and I never tired of examining every detail of the shiny new bicycles in the window, dreaming of the day when we would own one.

Sometimes we made a special trip just to get barber-shop haircuts. I liked the good-smelling tonic the barber rubbed in my hair.

Most of these trips were made in our Model T. But sometimes it was by horse and wagon, when we rode high on top a load of oats to be ground into meal at the elevator.

W hen winter came, our car was parked in the shed and the wagon box was transferred from its running gear to the chassis of the bobsled.

One time, two days before Christmas, dad said he was going into Latimer and asked if we boys would like to go along. We eagerly said yes. We washed behind our ears, put on clean shirts and overalls, and bundled up against the cold. Dad slipped on large horsehide mittens to keep his hands warm while holding the reins. To pacify our little brother, who could not go along, we promised to bring home a surprise.

As we set out, dad permitted us to tie our coaster behind the bobsled. It was great fun, with both of us sitting on the little sled, lurching along behind through the snowy ruts and drifts, trying to stay upright.

We enjoyed this sport for about the first two miles. By then, however, our fingers were tingling with the cold, and our toes felt like small, frozen potatoes inside our boots. So we and our sled were loaded onto the bobsled for the last mile into town.

Turning onto Main Street, with its few shops clustered near the Farmers Elevator, we were eager for the day's next adventure.

We tied the team to the hitching rail beside Dohrman's store, then went inside. The double doors closed behind us, a bell tinkling its familiar greeting. The warmth and fragrance of the big store decorated for Christmas engulfed us.

My brother and I made straight for the floor grate over the furnace, where we dropped our wet mittens to dry and soaked up some of the welcome heat ourselves.

We then headed for the toy display. There was a little steam engine that really worked, as well as an electric train and a toy drag line. A paint box and sketch pad and a toy sewing machine also captured our admiration.

The good smells from the grocery department at the back of the store soon drew us away from the toys. It had been a long time since our noon meal and everything looked good to us.

We lingered longingly over the cookies, the glass jars of candies—chocolates, jelly beans, orange slices, candy canes, and peanut brittle—along with the boxes of colorful hard candies that appeared only at Christmas. Boxes of fragrant apples and a crate of oranges added to the aroma.

Mr. Dohrman must have heard the growl of our empty stomachs for he selected two beautiful apples and gave one to each of us with a friendly wink and a "Merry Christmas."

With our hunger somewhat appeased my brother and I got down to the serious business of selecting gifts we could afford for the family.

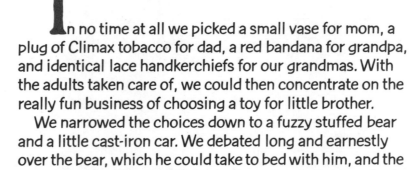

In no time at all we picked a small vase for mom, a plug of Climax tobacco for dad, a red bandana for grandpa, and identical lace handkerchiefs for our grandmas. With the adults taken care of, we could then concentrate on the really fun business of choosing a toy for little brother.

We narrowed the choices down to a fuzzy stuffed bear and a little cast-iron car. We debated long and earnestly over the bear, which he could take to bed with him, and the car, with which he could play in the summertime on the roads we would make for him. Finally, we decided on the car _and_ the bear. This used up all our coins, so we made a gentleman's agreement to postpone gifts for each other until next Christmas.

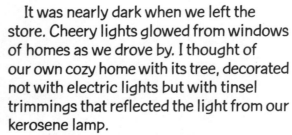

It was nearly dark when we left the store. Cheery lights glowed from windows of homes as we drove by. I thought of our own cozy home with its tree, decorated not with electric lights but with tinsel trimmings that reflected the light from our kerosene lamp.

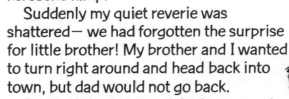

Suddenly my quiet reverie was shattered— we had forgotten the surprise for little brother! My brother and I wanted to turn right around and head back into town, but dad would not go back.

Suddenly dad stopped the horses and climbed out of the sled. He waded through the snow to a solitary tree and reached up into its bare branches. Returning to the sled, he presented us with an empty bird's nest.

Little brother was delighted with his "surprise" and placed it in our Christmas tree, where he gazed at it until bedtime, dreaming of its former tenants.

The Giving Heart

LOIS RAND

Have you read a new Christmas story in 1987? Or are you rereading an old favorite? Have you ever wondered why some stories fade after one reading and others last for years?

Any time of year, there's nothing like a good story. It tugs at your heart and shows you the truth about the world and yourself. It is retold and reread. It may be revised, revamped, translated, even mangled—over and over, round and round. Why is this? Because in it we see what is real.

Storytelling deals both with fact and with fantasy. If a tale tells the truth in a special way, we take it to ourselves and it becomes a classic. It endures.

The First Christmas Classics

Two of the best known and most-loved classics come from the mind of God, the ultimate storyteller, by way of his servants Matthew and Luke. We read them every Christmas. Each is just a few sentences long, yet together they recount the central act of God's love toward us and the human response to that love. They are the seedbed for all other genuine Christmas stories. They reveal to us pure generosity. That remarkable word, *generosity*, is derived from the word for family and describes the unselfish giving for others we love, which is a true family hallmark.

Luke's account of God's incredible generosity toward us in sending his Son, the baby born in the Bethlehem stable, reveals true love to the world. We see in this simple story the profound truth of God's coming in an unexpected way to undeserving yet very needy creatures, whom God loves as God's family.

Matthew has written the sequel, describing through the Magi a special human response to God's generosity. The Wise Men from the East ignored the tedium and dangers of a long journey to bring not only their most precious possessions, but also themselves, their homage and adoration, to the child King lying in the manger.

These bits of God's Word, these two classic stories, are the seeds of a Christmas culture grown up across the globe through all the succeeding years. And, as is the way with good stories, they have undergone universal adoption. Fragments of them have been grafted onto tales from pagan cultures, interpreted or misinterpreted, adjusted, diminished or expanded according to local usage or historical whim. From this process have come hundreds of tales we consider to be Christmas classics.

The St. Nicholas Legends

Perhaps the best known tales have evolved through the centuries since St. Nicholas was Bishop of Myra in Turkey during the fourth century. He was acclaimed as a miracle worker, a champion of the people, and the protector of innocents. He is reported to have rescued victims of injustice and children in need through gifts of money given at critical moments. He liked to spirit a purse of money through a window into a room in the dead of night, for he believed true charity should be anonymous so the recipients would give all thanks and honor to the Christ.

No written history supports these early tales about St. Nicholas, but they were passed along from parents to children. Because St. Nicholas died in December, gifts given in memory of his generosity became linked with Christmas. As his story reached to other lands and generations, it gradually provided us with many variations on the theme of generosity in the name of Christ.

As the tales spread, a counter-theme crept in, one which was not present in the stories about St. Nicholas himself and certainly not in the original Christmas stories told by Luke and Matthew. This counter-theme was one of retribution for sin and, perhaps, was included as a teaching device or a contrivance to control behavior. Stories developed that described gift-giving in terms of rewards such as candy, fruit, and gifts in return for goodness, and punishments such as switches, chains, and ashes in return for naughtiness.

When we look at the persistent overlay of these ideas through the years, we see that they put in reverse order the basic and significant truths of God's Christmas message to the world. The gleaming core of the original story was the lavish but undeserved generosity from God to a needy world, followed by loving and giving human behavior from those who had been blessed and cleansed by this great gift of the Savior.

The St. Nicholas story, as well as the many legends growing from it, have in effect developed a split personality through the years. Two beings are present, one Christ-like and one Satan-like, with the various characteristics of each. It is true that we face the presence of both good and evil in the world, that we need to be rescued from the evil and restored by the grace and goodness of God. It is also true that a perverse part of the human heart loves to shudder at threatened dangers. The result has been a flourishing of Christmas legends that popularize the dark element through such characters as Doppelganger, Old Nick, Black Jack, and even Tomte Gubbe. You have met them and, no doubt, have been entertained by them.

The loving element, true to the first Christmas story, has been introduced through such popular figures as Sanct Herr, St. Nick, Sinterklaas, and Kriss Kringle (the loftiest of all, from *Christkindl*, the Christ child). And finally, of course, came Santa Claus, a phonetic variation of St. Nicholas, who embodies within his legends a strange mixture of abundant giving and the idea that a person must be good to deserve it!

So a revised body of Christmas tales, classics of a sort, have been welcomed and accepted, with appropriate local variations, all over the globe. Many of these emphasize a kind of overflowing human generosity, yet they often ignore the source of the whole idea. We find ourselves struggling to bring the truth of the original Christmas classics into focus against such a tide.

However, not all Christmas stories grow by hearsay and across centuries. Some are crafted of whole cloth by perceptive writers who enlighten and entertain as they return to the basic truths of Matthew and Luke. Among such tales, some become classics cherished for their insight and beauty.

Four of these are among those you may read this Christmas. Although they are not all meant to be "religious," they all speak about human nature and the nature of God. Three of them borrow from the Magi to portray the response of human beings to unselfish love. The fourth addresses the same issue by examining the negative side of this truth. They all say something important about generosity. They all deserve a look and a rereading as you think of generosity—God's and yours—this Christmas.

The Other Wise Man

A Presbyterian minister and professor of English at Princeton, Henry Van Dyke (1852-1933), dipped directly into Matthew's account of the Magi for his inspiration. "The Other Wise Man" tells of an imagined fourth Wise Man, Artaban of Persia, who, like his three friends, watches for the star and plans to follow it to the new King. In preparation, he sells all his goods and purchases a sapphire, a ruby, and a pearl to bring as gifts.

But events conspire against Artaban. He misses the rendezvous with his friends because he stops to help a sick stranger on the road. He has to sell the sapphire to buy a fresh horse and supplies so he can go on alone.

Arriving at Bethlehem after a long, lonely trek, he finds his friends have come and gone. He is in time, however, to see Herod's soldiers invade Bethlehem, intent on killing all its babies. To protect a young mother and her child, he gives the ruby to a searching squad leader, but he agonizes within himself, "I have spent for man that which was meant for God."

Artaban's fervor to find the King takes him during the next 33 years all through the Mideast and at last brings him to Jerusalem just in time to learn of a pending execution. Tidbits of information he has gathered through the years convince him that the sentenced prisoner is the one he has been seeking. Hastening toward Calvary in hopes of using the remaining pearl as a ransom, he is stopped by the pleas of a girl being sold into slavery. In compassion he gives the pearl to set her free. Just at that moment he is mortally injured by debris from an earthquake.

In his dying moments, Artaban hears a voice say, "Inasmuch as thou hast done it unto one of the least of these my brethren, thou hast done it unto me." His treasures are accepted, and he at last finds the King. Having lived his life with a commendable hope that has been continually frustrated, Artaban has known much grief. In the end, however, the realization of his hope comes in a totally unexpected way.

Van Dyke's tale is improbable, moralistic, and, some say, even cloying. But it is a captivating account not only of commitment to one's belief, but also of generosity towards others in need.

The words of Jesus heard by Artaban at the story's end assure us that there is a suitable way for us to respond to God's generosity—not by gold, frankincense, myrrh, or even jewels brought to the manger, but by loving care of those in need.

A Christmas Carol

Many would choose "A Christmas Carol" by Charles Dickens first if asked to name a Christmas classic. It has been read and dramatized countless times since its English author wrote it in 1843. Tiny Tim and Scrooge have become genuine folk figures. It is an entertaining and dramatic story, and it tells the truth largely by focusing on the negative.

Dickens describes Scrooge as "a squeezing, wretched, grasping, scraping, clutching, covetous old sinner." Despite being surrounded by folks filled with goodwill and holiday joy, his view as he bends over his balance sheet is, "Out upon Merry Christmas!"

Do you remember how he learns? It is through a set of frightening dreams; many of us would wish that the path away from selfishness were so simple as a night of dreams.

Scrooge's dead partner, Marley, reflects on his own misspent life and rues his past blindness: "Not to know that any Christmas spirit working kindly in its little sphere . . . will find its mortal life too short for its vast means of usefulness." What should Scrooge think, hearing a lament on the very traits he himself embodies?

His dream surveys Christmases past, present, and to come. There's his old boss, Fezziwig: "The happiness he gives is quite as great as if it cost a fortune." As a young man, Scrooge had observed this in Fezziwig, but he himself has long since forgotten the happiness of others.

There are the Cratchits: "They were not well-dressed, but they were happy, grateful, pleased with one another, and contented with the time." Scrooge observes his employee, Bob Cratchit, regularly, yet he has neglected to express in his own life any gratitude for everyday blessings.

There is the preview of Scrooge's own death, with nobody taking notice, and of Tiny Tim's, with a loving family remembering the pleasure it has been to care for their handicapped boy. Scrooge dreads what he sees as his own future, one without love or hope.

Out of these negative images, Dickens works a change in the heart of Scrooge, a change that results first in practical action (for certainly Scrooge is a practical man!). He sends a Christmas turkey to the Cratchits and raises Bob Cratchit's salary. Best of all, the change of heart lasts. Many external circumstances remain, but "his own heart laughed, and that was enough for him. . . . Henceforth, it was always said of him that he knew how to keep Christmas well."

Dickens lays before us the idea that generosity begins with an unselfish attitude, and it brings joy.

The Gift of the Magi

Della and Jim are the characters introduced by the popular American writer, William Sydney Porter (1862-1910), who wrote under the pen name O. Henry. "The Gift of the Magi" is his most famous short story. It describes a young couple, very much in love and poor.

It is Christmas Eve. Della has one dollar and 87 cents, but she is determined to give Jim a gift to show her love. By cutting and selling to a wigmaker her glorious, long brown hair, she is able to buy a platinum chain for Jim's heirloom watch. She can scarcely wait for his return.

But her joy is interrupted when Jim sees her shorn head, for he has pawned his watch to buy her a pair of tortoise-shell jewelled combs!

O. Henry's deftness in giving this little plot its wry twist leaves Della and Jim with their ridiculously useless gifts, but with an expression of love far greater than either of them had planned. In a last aside to the reader, the author comments that Della and Jim's sacrifice of their

greatest treasures, each for the other, shows the wisdom of the Magi.

This is a truth to ponder. Love produces selflessness, which finds its expression in generosity beyond all odds.

Amahl and the Night Visitors

A relatively new work, "Amahl and the Night Visitors," is an opera that premiered on television Christmas Eve, 1951. Its charming music is inextricably entwined with its enchanting story, both written by Gian-Carlo Menotti (b. 1911). And it has already found its place among the classics.

Menotti has said that the memories of his childhood Christmases in Italy, with their emphasis on the Magi's gifts to the Christ child, helped to focus his thoughts on the theme for this tale.

The crippled shepherd boy, Amahl, and his poor mother receive into their humble home three kings seeking shelter on their way to see a newborn child, whom they revere

as a greater King than they.

During the night, the mother is caught trying to steal from the kings' wealth to help her child. In response, the kings explain to her that the child they seek does not need their gold, but will build his kingdom on love.

The mother, saying she has wanted all her life to find such a love, wishes she had something to send the child as a gift. Amahl offers his crutch ("Who knows, he may need one!"), and is suddenly healed of his lameness.

The kings, convinced this is a sign from the holy child, invite Amahl to come with them to give his gift and bring his own thanks to the child.

While emphasis is often placed on Amahl's miraculous healing when he puts the child first, there is also another miracle, the changed heart of the mother as she responds to the story of the Christ child's love.

The experience of Amahl and his mother reminds us that love offered begets love in return. Such love is the basis for a selflessness that prompts generosity.

All of these eloquent Christmas tales focus sharply on the giving heart, moved by love to put others first. Such was the love of God in giving the original Christmas gift. Such was the love expressed in the life and death of the Gift himself. And such is a faithful human reflection of God's love in our lives.

This Christmas, when we read again the accounts of Luke and Matthew, we might also delve into these other classics that grew from that first story. They can help refine our thoughts about the nature of giving, about what is cause and what is consequence.

God, the great storyteller, is also the great giving heart who has lavished abundant gifts on us, his earthly family. Thinking of the generosity of the giver and the glory of his gift of the Christ child is the reason to celebrate Christmas. We rejoice in this offer of rescue from our sinful state and restoration to the family.

Part of that celebration is savoring the truths told in the old stories. And part of that celebration is responding with giving hearts, which honor the giver and the gift, and as a consequence lead to generosity, which brings joy to us and to all we love and help in the Christ child's name.

Angels in Christmas Literature and Art

RUTH STOPHEL NEWSOME

I am Gabriel, who stands in the presence of God, and was sent to speak to you" (Luke 1:19). Gabriel, the first angel of Christmas, had just given Zachariah the news that he and his wife, Elizabeth, would have a son. Zachariah did not believe the angel, as he and Elizabeth were both of advanced years. Gabriel assured Zachariah that it was indeed true. But because he did not believe, Zachariah would be struck dumb until the child was born. Immediately Zachariah's lips were sealed and remained so until the baby was born. At that time Zachariah confirmed what Elizabeth had said by writing on a slate, "His name is John" (Luke 1:63), and immediately he could speak again.

We find Christmas angels in many places—in the biblical account, in our Christmas music, on our greeting cards, in our treasured Christmas stories, on our trees, and in our nativity figures made from clay, corn shucks, handcarved wood, fine porcelain, or other materials. The angels of Christmas, whether biblical or from our Christian tradition, add much to the spirit and meaning of Christmas, as well as to our celebration of Christmas.

Gabriel is an archangel. We read in the Bible of several occasions when Gabriel served God on earth. Tradition maintains that Gabriel is the one who walked with the three men in the fiery furnace and protected them from harm, the one who saved Daniel from the lions' jaws, and one of the three who visited Abraham. Gabriel, sometimes regarded as the angel of humanity, has been described as the "most beautiful of angels."

Gabriel was also the bearer of God's message to Mary. Luke tells us that the angel went to Mary and greeted her by saying, "Hail, highly favored one, the Lord is with you; blessed are you among women" (Luke 1:28). This account in Luke is our only record of Gabriel's visit to Mary; and although it gives us all the essential information, it is a brief ac-

The innocence of childhood is captured in this delightful figurine, styled after a drawing by Berta Hummel.

count and lacks descriptive words. For centuries people have wondered: Where was Mary? How did the angel appear before her? What did the angel carry? What was Mary wearing? How was the angel dressed? The words of Luke have inspired artists, poets, and writers for hundreds of years to fill in the details of this astonishing event with their own interpretation. The annunciation, or announcement to Mary, is the real beginning of the Christmas story and has been a favorite subject of artists for centuries.

Mary is generally shown seated. German artist Matthias Grunewald's three panel altarpiece, painted in approximately 1515, shows Mary in a chapel. Dutch artist Hubert Van Eyck's treatment places Mary in what appears to be a wealthy Flander's home. In *The Annunciation to the Virgin,* painted in 1430 by Fra Angelico, Mary is shown quietly reading, as she is also in a 1447 painting of the annunciation by Peter Cristus.

Gabriel is often shown dressed in red robes or with a red mantel over a robe of gold. In art Gabriel sometimes carries a scepter, sometimes wears a crown, is usually large winged, and often has his right hand extended. In early paintings Gabriel is the dominant figure, with Mary depicted as very submissive. During the fourteenth century this began to change. Mary became more dominant; Gabriel was shown sometimes carrying a lily and sometimes kneeling before Mary. This shift in emphasis was probably an indication of the changing feeling of the church, placing Mary in a more exalted position.

Tradition holds that Gabriel next appeared to Joseph. Joseph was troubled at the news that Mary was to have a baby. According to the first chapter of Matthew, an angel of the Lord appeared to Joseph and assured him that the child was conceived of the Holy Spirit.

After the birth of Jesus, an angel again appeared to Joseph, warning him to take Mary and the baby to Egypt for safety (Matthew 2:13). Tradition tells us that Gabriel accompanied the holy family on this trip. We know that after the death of Herod, Joseph again was visited by an angel (Matthew 2:19), and it was then that Joseph, Mary, and Jesus returned to Nazareth, thus fulfilling prophecy.

According to the Bible, on the night Jesus was born the angel of the Lord appeared to shepherds watching their flocks. Although we are not told specifically that this angel was again Gabriel, some believe that it was. Others believe that it was another of the archangels, Raphael. Raphael is known as the guardian angel and is believed to have been, along with Gabriel, one of the angels who visited Abraham.

After the angel spoke to the shepherds, "Do not be afraid, for behold, I bring you good tidings of great joy" (Luke 2:10), we are told that the angel was joined by a multitude of the heavenly host who joined in praise to God, saying, "Glory to God in the highest."

In the story, "The Christmas Angel," by Henry Van Dyke, a man dreamed he saw angels gathered in conversation. The angels had been on various missions to earth and were discussing the sad state of affairs there. One angel, Michael, archangel and defender of heaven, would cure the world's evils with the sword. Another angel, whom the dreamer knew to be the archangel Uriel, spirit of the Sun, clearest in vision and deepest in wisdom of all the angels, would give the good more wisdom. With this he was sure that all folly would fall away. The archangel Raphael, however, said that until the children of God learned to love each other and to help each other there would be no peace. Even though Raphael knew that love was the answer, he did not know how this could be accomplished.

As the others puzzled over this, a clear voice came ringing, "I know it; I know it; I know it." And then a young angel appeared, a little child with flying hair of gold. This young angel flew among them and said, "Man shall be made like God because the Son of God shall become a man." The young angel went on to say, "By suffering, he will understand the meaning of all pain and sorrow and will be able to comfort those who cry, and his tears will be for the healing of sad hearts and those who are healed will learn for his sake to be kind to others."

The young angel told them that no heart open to love could help loving him who loved enough to die. They asked the young angel how he knew all this. His reply was, "I am the Christmas angel and today is Christmas Day on earth and today the Son of God is born of a woman, and now I must fly quickly to bring the good news to those chosen to receive them." With this the young angel, followed by the others, flew and flew until they came to a field where the shepherds watched their flocks in the quiet night.

Selma Lagerlof in "The Holy Night" tells of a hardhearted and cruel shepherd, who nevertheless was moved to compassion when he came upon an innocent child in danger of freezing. Giving the child a soft sheepskin with which to keep warm, he saw what he had not seen before—a ring of silver-winged angels, each holding a stringed instrument and singing of the birth of the Savior. According to the story, the angels come down to earth each Christmas and are there for anyone who would see them.

We are not told in the Bible that an angel went with the shepherds to the manger, but this has been painted numerous times. For example, in the late 1400s Italian artist Carlo Crivelli painted an angel guiding a shepherd to the manger while a band of angels hovered overhead. Marcellus Cofferman's *Adoration of the Shepherds* shows angels kneeling by the manger, as well as angels singing overhead.

For the Linen Guild in Florence, Fra Angelico painted a group of 12 angels using musical instruments to praise the newborn babe. Fra Angelico's painting of the angels was so splendid that it was said he must have actually seen the angels in heaven in order to have painted them with such radiance. Angels playing music were also depicted in a section of an altarpiece carved in wood by Arnt between 1483 and 1492 for the Church of St. Nicholas in Calcar, Germany. In the late fifteenth century, Piero della Francesca painted angels strumming lutes and singing at the nativity. In an effort to downplay any supernatural dimension, he depicted the angels without

(left) This porcelain angel with censor is a reproduction of an eighteenth century Neapolitan creche figure.
(right) Angels are often depicted with musical instruments, as is this papier-mâché angel from Italy.

(left) Reminiscent of Tazewell's "Littlest Angel" is this angel from Hallmark's Little Gallery collection.
(right) This graceful angel reflects the outstanding beauty of the Loretta Hines Howard creche figure collection.

halo or wings.

Prior to the middle of the fourth century, angels always were shown without wings. At one time, the church forbade the depiction of angels in any form. This edict was eventually relaxed. But in the early Renaissance period, angels were shown as severe-looking men. Gradually this image evolved to show them as young boys with curls, and then the feminine appearance we see pictured today became common.

The subject of angels continues to fascinate people, especially at Christmastime when angels figure so prominently in the gospel story. Through the centuries and around the world, artists have tried to capture their own personal vision of these heavenly beings. As a result, the figures often reflect the background of the artists. The angels by Spanish, Dutch, Oriental, and Italian masters all have their own unique look. This is evident in the nativity sets made by the Brasstown Carvers in the mountains of North Carolina. Handcarved from holly wood, the figures reflect the facial features of the mountain people.

The re-creation of a live nativity scene is credited to St. Francis of Assisi. In Greccio, Italy, in 1223, St. Francis brought together village people and animals around a manger in which a young child lay so that he might make the Christmas story more real to them.

Following St. Francis' example, the custom of setting up crib scenes spread. In 1291 marble figures of the nativity created by Arnolfo di Cambri were placed in the Prescipio Chapel in the Church of Santa Maria. We do not know specifically that angels were a part of this grouping. However, in 1344 Margaretha Ebner of the Dominican Order recorded that she had received from Vienna a depiction of the Christ child in a cradle surrounded by four little golden angels.

From its beginning in churches, the custom of nativity scenes spread to homes and castles. In 1567 angels were included in an inventory of items belonging to the Duchess of Amalfi. In 1734, King Don Carlo III of Naples stressed that he wanted the nativity angels to "breathe with heavenly beauty." One of the most elaborate nativity settings that we know about was created for King Charles III of Naples in the eighteenth century; it featured both cupids and elegant angels. The Archduchess of Bavaria, Marie Von Stormack, is known to have made clothes for flexible, jointed nativity figures, including angels.

One of the most extensive collections of nativity figures in the world is the Loretta Hines Howard collection at the Metropolitan Museum of Art in New York. This collection numbers some 200 figures and features angels of outstanding beauty. There are numerous cherubs and glorious angels in this grouping, many of them having come from "The Adoration of Angels" formerly owned by Eugenio Catello of Naples. This grouping came to Loretta Howard's attention in 1952 when it was exhibited in Paris. After three years of negotiations, she purchased the grouping. Then in 1964 she donated it to the museum as a part of their permanent collection. For many years Howard personally supervised the setting up of the museum's Angel Tree each Christmas season, using figures from the collection.

Of children, Charles Dickens once said, "They are the angels of God in disguise. . . . His glory still gleams in their eyes." Perhaps that is why we often see angels represented as children. Many of the drawings of Sister M. Innocentia (Berta Hummel) depict angels with the innocence of children. These drawings have been reproduced in many mediums, including the beloved Hummel figurines. Among those drawings that have been reproduced as figurines is one of childlike angels guarding the infant Jesus, a beautiful nativity set.

In the last several years, figures of children dressed as if they might be participating in a church Christmas play have become popular illustrations of the Christmas story. The Hallmark Little Gallery nativity by Mary Hamilton is one example. The youthful faces of dressed-up children portray Mary, Joseph, the Wise Men, the shepherds, and the "joyful angel."

Another nativity sculpture with children as the participants is the popular Precious Moments grouping, patterned after the drawings of artist Sam Butcher. The appealing look of childlike faith and wonder makes this crèche treasured by many. In addition to the holy family, Wise Men, and shepherds, there are several angels in the grouping.

No medium has been used more than painting to show the angels of Christmas. But we also cherish a number of stories that describe the role of angels. In addition to Van Dyke's "Christmas Angel," a beloved story is Charles Tazewell's "Littlest Angel." The Littlest Angel was only four when he arrived in heaven and was having a hard time becoming acclimated. At last, the Understanding Angel talked with him, and the Littlest Angel's dearest possession on earth, a wooden box filled with a small boy's treasures—two smooth stones, a butterfly, a skyblue egg, and the limp leather strap that had once served as a collar for his dog—was brought to heaven for him. Having this box made so much difference; he was much happier and better behaved. Then all of the angels of heaven became busy making wonderful gifts for

(left) The popular Precious Moments figurines feature a nativity set, which includes this adoring angel.
(right) Handcarved from holly wood by the Brasstown Carvers, the face of this angel resembles the mountain people.

God's Son. The Littlest Angel also wanted to give a gift. He thought of and rejected numerous ideas. At last, the Littlest Angel decided to give the Christ child the things he had treasured most in life—his precious box and all its contents. He slipped his gift into place with all the others and then was dismayed to see how rough it looked there among all the splendid gifts. If he could have, he would have retrieved it; but God's hand reached out and came to rest on the Littlest Angel's gift. And God said, "Of all the gifts of all the angels . . . this small box pleases me most." As the Littlest Angel watched, the box began to glow with a blinding radiance. Then it rose until it spanned the firmament and shone down over a stable in Bethlehem.

Angels of Christmas also appear in the music of the season. "Ava Maria" by Schubert tells Mary's story and is considered by many to be one of the most moving melodies ever written.

"Hark! The Herald Angels Sing" was written by Charles Wesley in 1739, but it was inspired by something that happened when Charles was only nine years old. Charles had contracted a very bad cold and had been told, despite his keen disappointment, that he could not go with the rest of the family to the Christmas Eve midnight church service. As Charles, with tears in his eyes, snuggled down into his blanket alone, the night seemed filled with frightening sounds. Suddenly Charles heard voices singing, voices that seemed to come from the sky. He remembered how the angels sang on the first Christmas and he thought they were singing again. Later, of course, he realized that what he had heard was the church choir singing, their voices carrying in the stillness of the night. But the memory stayed with him and inspired what has been called "the most beautiful English hymn ever written."

Many of our Christmas carols come from England. But one American carol is "It Came Upon the Midnight Clear," sometimes called "The Angel's Song," written in 1849 by Edmund Hamilton Sears. Sears knew that many of his congregation were sad or disheartened, in need of some special word of encouragement. He hoped his poem telling about the night the angels sang would give them a special feeling of the glory of the Savior's birth. Little did he realize when he wrote his verse that it would become one of our most-loved Christmas songs.

Another American Christmas carol, "O Little Town of Bethlehem," was written by Phillip Brooks in 1868 and was inspired by his visit to Bethlehem on Christmas Eve three years earlier. He gave the poem to his church organist and asked him to set it to music. The organist, Lewis Redner, was deeply touched by the words of the poem; all week he tried to compose a fitting tune. On Christmas Eve, the night before the tune was needed, he went to bed troubled because he still had been unable to find a tune he felt would be worthy of the poem. Then as he fell asleep, he dreamed he heard the angels singing. He awakened, startled by the reality of his dream, and, as quickly as he could, wrote down the tune he had heard. That is the tune we sing today.

The angels of Christmas, whether portrayed by sculptors, painters, writers, or composers, add a joyous note to our celebration of Jesus' birth. For it was an angel who brought the message: "There is born to you this day . . . a Savior." And it was a host of angels who sang: "Glory to God in the highest, and on earth peace, good will to men!" (Luke 2:11, 14). Regardless of the medium used to portray angels, the message of these heavenly beings rings true and glad: To us is born a child who brings peace and goodwill on earth, all through the year but especially at Christmas.

Our Christmas

Christmas Eve _____

_____

_____

_____

Christmas Day _____

_____

_____

_____

Christmas Worship _____

_____

_____

Christmas Guests   Christmas Gifts

_____   _____

_____   _____

_____   Christmas   _____

_____   Photo   _____

_____   _____

_____   _____

_____   _____

_____